Architecture, Language,
and Meaning

Approaches to Semiotics

49

MOUTON PUBLISHERS · THE HAGUE · PARIS · NEW YORK

Approaches to Semiotics

49

MOUTON PUBLISHERS · THE HAGUE · PARIS · NEW YORK

Architecture, Language, and Meaning

Architecture, Language, and Meaning

*The Origins of the Built World
and its Semiotic Organization*

Donald Preziosi

MOUTON PUBLISHERS · THE HAGUE · PARIS · NEW YORK

ISBN: 90-279-7828-X
Cover design by Jurriaan Schrofer
© 1979, Mouton Publishers, The Hague, The Netherlands
Printed in the Netherlands

Because perception and action take place in continuous dependence upon the environment, they cannot be understood without an understanding of that environment itself.

Ulric Neisser, *Cognition and Reality*, 1976, 183.

Preface

The aim of the present volume is the elaboration of a semiotic perspective on the problems surrounding the origins and evolution of the built environment. The present text is an arrested moment in an ongoing research program begun in 1970 at Yale University, continued since 1973 at MIT, and since 1977 in Ithaca. Some of this work was reported on elsewhere (D. Preziosi 1979a). The following represents the application of the current results of that research program to the growing body of important speculation on the question of human cultural origins.

At the present time, the energies of researchers in a wide variety of disciplines, from cognitive anthropology to zoosemiotics, are being directed to the elaboration of theoretical models for sociocultural origins and evolution. One of the most important frontiers currently being explored in the panoply of concerns regarding the nature and organization of human semiotic activity is the area of *architectonic theory*—the set of methods and perspectives currently being brought to bear on the evidence for systematicity in the significative organization of built environments. The increasing urgency of this task, discussed in the Preface below, is augmented by increasing indications regarding the systemic correlativities in the design features of architectonic and linguistic systems: as a result of the recent maturity of architectonic theory and analysis, we are now in a position to begin to explore both broadly and concretely, the nature of the similarities and differences between these two fundamental panhuman sign-systems, redressing the isolation of sophistication of insight in verbal semiotics.

While architectonic theory today operates from a broadly holistic perspective on the built environment in its totalities, this has not always been the case, and for generations the study of the built environment had been fragmented into a variety of foci and subject matter, and a variety of methods and conceptual domains, from 'architectural history' to environmental psychology to interactional and spatiokinetic analysis. What has lucidly emerged over the past decade is the view that only a holistic and integral perspective on the entire set of significative environmental behaviors can make sense of the synechdochal indications of systematicity in the organization of the variety of modalities in the visual realm. It has additionally become apparent that it is only in such a framework that we may begin to more fully understand the nature of verbal semiosis, and its embeddedness among the network of sign-systems defining and defined by culture.

The present volume is embedded in the theoretical perspectives on the built environment elaborated during the present decade in the aforementioned research project, and constitutes a provisional attempt to elaborate a pansemiotic framework for the interactive origins and evolution of cultural semiosis. As such, the present study is necessarily incomplete and provisional, despite its interactional and comparative focus. We are only at the beginning of a new and exciting phase of semiotic inquiry, and any study such as the present one constitutes more of an opening to dialogue than a set of formulaic pronouncements. Purely and simply, we need to know considerably more from a variety of disciplinary perspectives to be able to address the issues raised below in a more than delicate and tentative manner. In particular, both semiotic inquiry and the study of perceptual and cognitive psychology need to become increasingly sensitive to the overlapped nature of their concerns: much of the recent work in the latter area has profoundly important implications for the development of semiotics, and it is patently the case that all semiotic analysis bears implications for the future development of perceptual psychology. The study of human semiosis and perception comprise compatible and complementary (and supplementary) perspectives on the constructive orchestration of meaning. In the writer's view, both semiotics and perceptual psychology rightly reject the role of viewer or observer or decoder or reader as a passive cryptographer and affirm that semiosis and perception are cyclic, temporal, and interactive activities oriented toward the significative construal and production of information. We may very well suggest, more than impressionistically, that in their fundamental mechanics they are metonymically related as two sides of the same coin, and metaphorically related by their equivalencies of process.

As saliently noted by Ulric Neisser in his important recent study (Neisser 1976:183), 'Because perception and action take place in continuous dependence upon the environment, they cannot be understood without an understanding of that environment itself'. The present volume has as one of its aims the portrayal of the systematicity of the built environment, and attempts to define a number of areas where the recent growth of architectonic inquiry may augment our understanding of the origins and evolution of human cognition.

The initial impetus for the present study was the occasion of an interdisciplinary graduate seminar conducted by the writer at MIT in 1975 on the origins of architecture, concurrent with the aforementioned research program on the semiotic analysis of built environments. The appearance of this volume itself runs concurrent with an analytic and taxonomic study of Paleolithic settlement remains as presently known, a study which has as one of its goals the elaboration of a typological framework for the comparative analysis of built environment formations in human history.

The research upon which the present book is based was supported in part by various grants and fellowships, including a fellowship from the National Endowment for the Humanities (1973-1974), and various supportive grants from the Department of the History of Art at Yale University. I am also grateful for the in-house leaves from the Department of Art and Architecture at MIT during 1973 and 1974 which enabled me to begin putting in order the accumulation of notes and data begun several years before. The initial impetus for the exploration of the issues discussed in the present volume and in concurrent writings came from the generous allowances of time offered by a Charles Eliot Norton Fellowship from Harvard University, and a Harvard Travelling Fellowship, during 1964-1966.

The number of persons whose interactions with the writer have affected the present study to its benefit is very great. Many colleagues, friends, and students have left an imprint on this book in direct and indirect ways, and it has often been the case that a chance remark or a brief conversational interaction has stimulated a train of thought which ultimately led to the clarification of the aims of this project. I must above all acknowledge the contributions of many students and friends in my graduate seminars at Yale and MIT whose lively, informed, and insightful conversations and enormous energies were crucial both in the launching of this project and in its continuation. My teachers at Harvard and my colleagues at Yale, MIT, and Cornell have been similarly generous with their time with someone perhaps overtly impatient to define the right questions to ask. The following list is partial, and I have tried to include all those with whom some (even momentary) personal interaction has affected the present report to its benefit:

Wayne Andersen, Stanford Anderson, Michael Bales, Keith Basso, Dwight Bolinger, Kwang-chih Chang, William Davenport, Philippe Dordai, Peter Eisenmann, Mario Gandelsonas, Paul Garvin, Charles Gates, Wladimir Godzich, Ernst Gombrich, Steven Grossberg, M. A. K. Halliday, Elmar Holenstein, Dell Hymes, Roman Jakobson, Hong-bin Kang, K. Lamberg-Karlovsky, Ik Jae Kim, George Kubler, Sydney Lamb, Shelagh Lindsey, Robert Manoff, Jonathan Matthews, Arden and Ulric Neisser, Sheldon Nodelman, Christian Norberg-Schulz, Werner Oechslin, Margaret Rogow, Irving Rouse, Lynne Rutkin, Nicholas Rykwert, Meyer Schapiro, Hal Scheffler, Vincent Scully, Thomas Sebeok, Edward Stankiewicz, Eléanor Steindler, Linda Suter, Alexander Tzonis, Paolo Valesio, Dora Vallier, and Linda Waugh. The text was patiently and expertly typed and composed by Mrs. Coraleen Rooney of Ithaca.

I am most particularly grateful to Linda Waugh and Roman Jakobson, whose continuing stimulation and support have clarified the direction of my questions.

Ithaca, New York   Donald Preziosi
December 1978

Contents

Contents

Overview: Linguistic and Architectonic Signs

In the semiotic task of revealing more clearly the place of language in communication, the study of nonverbal communication—and in particular the analysis of visual communication—has acquired today a fundamental urgency and importance.

The study of visual semiosis has been and still remains an enormously difficult task, for not only must we deal with complexities of organization which have no direct correlates in nonvisual sign-systems, but we must also carry forward the necessary extrication of visual semiotics from its verbocentric captivity without falling into any number of opposite extremes.

We cannot adequately understand any form of communication *in vacuuo*, for the various kinds of sign-systems evolved by humans have been designed from the outset to function in concert with each other in deictically-integrated ways, and it becomes increasingly clear that every code contains formative elements whose meaningfulness is ambiguous without indexical correlation to sign formations in other codes.

Human communication is characteristically *multimodal*. In the ongoing semiotic bricolage of daily life, we orchestrate and combine anything and everything at our disposal to create a significant world, or simply to get a message across. A semiotics of communicative events in their multimodal totality has yet to be born, and it will not come about until we have a more profound and complete understanding of the nature, organization, and operant behaviors of sign-systems other than verbal language.

The attempt to bring this about through the scientific superimposition of design features drawn from the study of verbal language upon other sign-systems has, by and large, been a failure. While it is true that much has been learned by such a procedure, the ultimate expected illumination has tended to be rather dim and fleeting in comparison to the energies expended, or, as more often has happened, the mute stones have remained mute.

This silence has induced some, for example the anthropologist Edmund Leach, to claim that it is only because all the things in an environment can be given lexical labels that we can recognize what they are—which is patently false (Leach 1976:33). As Michael Silverstein carefully reminds us, speech-acts are co-occurrent with events in distinct signaling media which together make up large-scale communicative events (Silverstein 1976:11-56).

Despite its truly unique powers and affordances, verbal language is not an active figure against a passive or static ground. This becomes increasingly clear the more we learn about the nature and organization of nonverbal sign-systems. One area of research which has grown up in recent years which uniquely promises to clarify the place of language in communication, and which has already served to collaterally illuminate certain features of the organization of linguistic systems themselves, is the area of architectonic analysis, concerned with the study of the system of the *built environment*—what has come to be called the *architectonic code.*

In part, the emergence of architectonic analysis as an integrated framework for the study of the built environment has become an inevitable and necessary result of the convergence of a series of perspectives on space- and place-making activity. While research elaborated over the past few decades under the rubrics of proxemics, kinesics, environmental psychology, man-environment relations, architectural history, body language, and perceptual psychology has had significant input into architectonic analysis over the past decade, not all of what each of these has had to say has been relevant. Each has been elaborated for different purposes, and each focusses upon a selected portion of the architectonic totality.

The first and most important approximation of such a synthesis came about during the 1960s with the emergence of 'architectural semiotics' and the quest for minimal meaningful units in architecture. Much of this work consisted of plugging in architecture to currently fashionable linguistic models, in the hope of specifying the nature of architectural 'deep structure' or of classifying architectural formations into phonemic, morphemic, or 'textual' unities.

But the plunge into the muddy waters of linguistic analogy brought little in the way of real illumination, and the 'semiotics of architecture' suffered additionally from a near-fatal flaw—*viz*. that 'architecture', as an autonomous system of signs, does not really exist except as a lexical label for certain arbitrarily restricted artifactual portions of the built environment, a picture artificially perpetuated by obsolescent academic departmentalization.

By hindsight, the attempt to develop a semiotics of buildings is rather like trying to understand the organization of language through a study of proper nouns. Inevitably, architectural semiotics rarely consisted of the analysis of the sum of copresent buildings in an environment—which itself would have made more sense—but instead largely concerned itself with arbitrarily selected portions of environmental arrays—prominent building types, for example, such as churches or domestic structures or factories or 'vernacular' construction.

The semiotics of buildings left us with an essentially incomplete and partial perspective on the phenomenon of architectonic semiosis, and it left us at a loss to deal with behaviors described for example by Marshall in the following African situation:

It takes the women only 3/4 of an hour to build their shelters, but half the time at least the women's whim is not to build shelters at all. In this case, they sometimes put up two sticks to symbolize the entrance of the shelters so that the family may orient itself as to which side is the man's and which the women's side of the fire. Sometimes they do not bother with the sticks (Marshall 1960:342).

The built environment is not merely equivalent to the sum of artifactual or made formations, but will normally include formations appropriated from a given landscape, as well as formations made solely by the relative deployment of bodies in space. This has nothing to do with technological capacity, nor is it a matter of code-switching. Nor is it peculiar to !Kung Bushmen, Australian aborigines, hunter-gatherers, or people living in warm climates, but is a property of any architectonic system.

The architectonic code incorporates the entire set of place-making orderings whereby individuals construct and communicate a conceptual world through the use of palpable distinctions in formation addressed to the visual channel, to be decoded spatio-kinetically over time. The proper scope of architectonics has come to be the entire range of such orderings, including all manners of space and place-making activities realized both artifactually and somatically—realized, in other words, through indirect or direct bodily instrumentality.

In an architectonic perspective, a room, a sewing machine in the corner of the room, a tree outside the window, and a mountain on the horizon, however else the latter three may function, may serve as sign-formations in an ordered and culture-specific system of architectonic signs. Moreover, even within the same code, formations may be as permanent as a pyramid or as momentary as a tent, a float in a parade, or a circle of elders assembling together in a meadow once a month.

Our traditional confusions on this point have stemmed from a misconstrual of the nature of the signing medium itself. In evident constrast to the situation with verbal language, where not only is the acoustic medium itself relatively homogeneous, the linguistic signals are themselves processed by the brain in different ways than nonlinguistic acoustic signals.[1] By contrast, architectonic signs are realized through what appears to be an impossibly complex hybrid of media. It would seem that the built environment can employ anything from frozen blocks of water in the Arctic to aggregates of steel and glass, from twigs and animal skins to mere clearings of a forest floor.

But it becomes clear that whether we are dealing with bamboo, concrete, ice, spotlights, lines in the sand, or positions around a lecture hall, we are dealing with geometric and material distinctions *per se* which, by address to the visual channel, are intended to cue the perception of distinctions in meaning, in culture-specific and code-specific ways. The architectonic code is a system of relationships manifested in material formations, and the medium of a given code is normally a mosaic of shapes, relative sizes, colors, textures, and materials—in other words, anything drawn from the entire set of material resources potentially offered by the planetary biosphere, including our own and other bodies.

The more we learn about architectonic systems, the more evident it becomes that each system employs only a selected portion of the potential resources of an ecology, and that the constraints upon the choice of materials are primarily semiotic and culture-specific.

In the broadest sense, communication may be said to involve, most centrally, the transmission of information regarding the perception of similarities and differences. Distinctions and disjunctions in formation are generically intended to cue the perception of similarities and differences in meaning. Meaningfulness is an aspect of a sign-system in its totality rather than being a black box appended in Rube Goldbergesque fashion to other black boxes, and nearly any formative distinction may be meaningful in some sense in a given code, and often in several senses at the same time.

The way each system does this is both code-specific and culture-specific. Meaningful distinctions in formation in one system may be nonsignificant in another code of the same type, or may be significant in different ways. It is evidently the case that any semiotic system is built upon a principle of relational invariance, and it is the task of any analysis to recognize and account for patterns of invariance in variation, and vice versa.

As a system of relationships, the architectonic code signifies conceptual associations through similarities and differences in visually-palpable formation. The amount of potential variation in a built environment may seem at first glance to be impossibly enormous. A glance down any street will reveal a multidimensional mosaic of colors, textures, shapes, sizes, and materials. But a closer look will reveal the presence of the same color applied to differently shaped formations, or of different colors applied to identically shaped formations, or of different colors applied to identically shaped formations which are of different relative sizes. Moreover, each of these permutations may be multiplied across contrastive materials, or across contrastive textures of the same materials.

What might have appeared initially as a visual continuum inevitably resolves itself into a highly complex multidimensional system of contrastive oppositions cued by disjunctions both in geometric and material formation. Moreover, what is done in one system with distinctions in coloration may be accomplished by geometric or morphological distinctions in another code. The analysis of any architectonic code must proceed principally within the specific parameters of organization of that code.

There is no human society which does not communicate, express, and represent itself architectonically. Moreover, there is not just one code spread in gradient diffusion around the globe, but as many codes as there are cultures, and more. The distribution of architectonic systems is not coterminous, however, with linguistic boundaries, and it has been found to be characteristically the case that two groups speaking the same language may contrast sharply in the nature and organization of their built environments. The converse also obtains.

The component units of an architectonic code defined by contrasts in geometric and material formation are not all meaningful in the same way. It has become evident in architectonic analysis over the past decade that an architectonic code comprises a hierarchically-ordered system of signs of various characteristic types.

In connection with a research program begun eight years ago at Yale and continued more recently at MIT, the analysis of large bodies of architectonic data from a variety of cultural contexts has illuminated the nature and interrelationships of architectonic sign types. A number of the salient implications of this research are discussed in the present volume; in general, the following picture of the organization of the architectonic code has emerged.[2]

It is now evidently the case that in any architectonic code the number of minimal significative units is limited, and that it is out of the syntagmatic and paradigmatic interaction of such units that the transfinite variety of architectonic formations in a built environment arises.

In addition, a code reveals the presence of several types of sign-formations or minimal units, related to each other in hierarchically-ordered sets. The largest directly-significant unit to be encoded as such, the *space-cell*, is itself built up of units which are principally meaningful in a systemic sense, and which serve to discriminate one cell from another. These units, or *forms*, as they have come to be called, consist of copresent spatial distinctive features of various types, as discussed below in Chapter IV.

Space-cells enter into tridimensional aggregates, called *matrices*, which, as sign-formations, comprise diagrams or patterns of syntagmatic cellular aggregation rather than larger cellular units, although it has become clear that in any code many such sign-patterns become temporarily fixed in characteristic association: this is subject, normally, to diachronic or diatopic variation.

Architectonic *forms*, while primarily significant in a systemic or sense-discriminative sense, may also serve sense-determinative or directly-significant functions under certain conditions in given codes. Thus, while the particular geometric configuration of a wall, for example, has a primary function in contributing to the contrastive discrimination of one cell from another, it may also, by virtue of its morphological characteristics, carry with it some form of direct signification. This may be over and above its material realization in terms of color, texture, absolute size, or physical material.

In this regard, architectonic and linguistic systems share a certain correlativity of systemic organization while contrasting most sharply with respect to the nature of formative units themselves. As a result of research over the past decade there is no longer any question that both systems are designed according to a principle of 'duality of patterning' or 'double articulation'.

But the architectonic code reveals a unique systemic feature not reflected except by weak approximation in nonvisual systems, which concerns the complexity of its material component, induced by the degree of potential variation in the material composition or realization of formal or geometric structure.

Whereas the material component of the system—the entire range of colors, textures, modularities of size as well as the range of materials employed—serves what is primarily a sense-discriminative function in the realization of formal or geometric units, the material parameters of a built environment offer a second major site for direct signification. The extraordinary range of these significative possibilities, which has no full analog in verbal language, has historically provided yet another block to our understanding of the nature of architectonic signification. The principal formative elements of the code—what constitutes its 'vocabulary', so to speak—consist of distinctions in formation *per se* beneath the material contextual variation explicit in architectonic objects.

Hence, while it has become clear that as a system the code is designed in ways which are correlative to the formative processes of linguistic systems, the multidimensional complexities of the code, manifest both spatially and temporally, are both unique and extraordinary.

It is now also clear that, in terms of functionality, both codes reveal correlative properties of organization. The question of architectonic meaning or function has not been resolved through the traditional misconstrual of 'architecture' as 'art', craft, engineering, theater, housing, frozen music, or some ingeneously clever way of writing texts in three dimensions. The study of the built environment through the offices of 'architectural history' has more often than not focussed upon only two or three of its functions—notably its contextually-referential or usage function, its aesthetic function, or its expressive function—and this way of dividing up the pie has been confounded with time- and culture-specific (and class-specific) notions of what buildings ought to do and how they ought to do it. The result has been a misconstrual of architectonic conation, expression, usage, territoriality or phaticism, and metasystemic or allusory functions.

Architectonic formations are inherently multifunctional in the sense that a given construct characteristically reveals, in code-specific ways, a variety of orientations upon the several component parts of a transmission, one or another of which may be in dominance at a given time over others which may be copresent. The built environment is no more an 'art' than is verbal language—except insofar as a given formation—of any usage type—may reveal a dominance of focus upon its own signalization, precisely paralleling the 'poetic' function of a given linguistic art.

The correlation of the functions of architectonic signs with characteristically dominant orientations upon the various copresent components in a transmission was proposed in rough form by the astute Czech theoretician Mukařovský in his 1938 monograph (Mukařovský 1978:236ff.), but it has not been until the past decade that the growth of architectonic analysis has matched his early insights. It is now clear that the functional horizons of architectonic formations correlate *systemically* with the picture of linguistic multifunctionality articulated by Jakobson (Jakobson 1956,

1960). Such a framework now finds additional salient application to other semiotic systems as well.

The picture of architectonic function and meaning is augmented by a unique property of the system, namely the relative permanence of its broadcast. Clearly, if a signal remains perceptually available, it becomes intersubjective property to many potential addressers and addressees. While some architectonic signals are more transitory than others in a given code, the range of relative permanence is in complementary contrast to the ephemerality of linguistic transmission. These contrastive properties confer unique and different advantages to each system. Verbal language and built environments interact in dynamic synchrony in complementary and supplementary fashion, as differentially-sustained components in the ongoing orchestration of meaning in daily life. The world that language builds is built in partnership with and in relationship to the relative object-permanence that architectonic sign-formations confer. By the same token, verbal language confers upon the built environment temporal variation in invariance.

Whatever the two codes share with respect to correlative processes of formation and transmission, they share by virtue of their both being panhuman sign-systems with partly-overlapping and mutually-implicative functions. The more we understand the particular parameters of organization of nonverbal codes such as the architectonic, the less will we be inclined to view the position of any one as an active figure against a static ground. This is not to deny the necessary operational paradox that any code can be employed, in communication, as a provisional metalanguage. Concomitantly, we shall be in a clearer position to understand how and why each copresent system provides its own particularly powerful perspective on the totalities of human experience, and the ways in which each such perspective necessarily implicates all others.

What distinguishes us from those of our primate relatives which we have allowed to survive over the past two million years is not the possession of any one code *per se*, but rather the globality of our intelligence in all modalities. It becomes increasingly embarrassing to assert that any one code is either phylogenetically or ontogenetically the template for all others. It is here that we must necessarily part company with semiotic theories which assert the primacy of any one code as a model for others. Our ancestors designed us with a predisposition toward the mixing of metaphors, knowing full well in their emergent wisdom that, if the only tool we had were a hammer, we would tend to treat everything as if it were a nail.

The aim of this book, then, is to explore the conditions for the emergence of this multimodal cognitive behavior as evidenced by the appearance and evolution of built environments in the human line, and to explore, by metonymic implication, the conditions for the concurrent emergence of verbal language itself.

NOTES

1. As discussed in R. Jakobson and L. R. Waugh (i.p., Chapter I).
2. See D. Preziosi (1979a) for a detailed discussion of this research project, which has been supported in part by the National Endowment for the Humanities and by research grants and other assistance from Yale University and MIT.

Introduction

PRELUDE

In September 1975 the New York Academy of Sciences sponsored a four day conference on the origins and evolution of language and speech, resulting in the publication of a volume containing nearly a hundred separate papers, discussion papers, and discussions of commentaries, representing a broad spectrum of perspectives on many aspects of the question of human language origins (Harnad, Steklis, and Lancaster, eds. 1976). Specialists in many areas, from linguistics to cognitive psychology and biology, brought to bear their particular expertise on the definition of common problems, and offered a wide variety of explanatory models addressed to linguistic origins and evolution.

In his concluding remarks to the conference, the anthropologist Robin Fox expressed a certain amount of dismay as to the lack of representation of speculation emanating from research in the social and anthropological sciences—a dismay particularly poignant when it is considered that language as we know it can only have had its origins and evolution in a context of increasing sociocultural complexity.

It might be added that in the light of a stress laid upon the importance of cross-modal communication and expression by a number of scholars, and particularly in the light of an occasional focus upon gestural signing, little patent consideration was given to the crucial importance of visual communication, both in affecting the course of, and in being itself modified by, the emergence of verbal language.

In part, this situation may be attributed to the fact that, in the study of visual semiosis, what has often passed for serious speculation has more often than not consisted of propaganda for one or another system of arbitrary classification, frequently based upon a literal borrowing of the methods and even data-language of other disciplines.

Nevertheless, the scientism so recently prevalent in visual semiotics has, in the past decade, begun to give way to an increasing body of systematic research from a variety of perspectives which bear upon the problem of defining targets of study through the patient and painstaking observation of visual signing and its phylogeny. At the present time, many lines of research have begun to show signs of convergence and imminent intersection, and it appears that the time may be ripe for a provisional consideration of what might be required of a truly holistic and relational perspective on the matrix of visual sign-systems at the core of human sociocultural behavior. Most notable in this regard is some recent work in perceptual and cognitive psychology which bears important implications for our understanding of the semiotic nature of perception itself.[1]

The present study is intended to suggest a number of tentative scenarios for the origins and evolution of communication in various modalities from a semiotic perspective. The purpose of the following is to define a number of salient issues which in my opinion need to be addressed by a semiotic theory (or cluster of theories) of human origins, in the light of recent findings on the organization of extra-verbal communication.

THE BUILT ENVIRONMENT

The built environment—the architectonic system—is the instrumentality *par excellence* among the set of activities constituting the 'tool kit' of *homo sapiens*. There is nothing elsewhere in the animal world to compare with this system of communication, representation and expression in power, subtlety, flexibility, and comprehensiveness. In human culture itself it is only rivaled by verbal language, with which it interacts in a complementary and mutually implicative manner. Together, language and the built world provide a complexly integrated matrix for action and interaction, a multimodal system of signs which serves as the primary template for the erection of the self and the collaborative consciousness.

The emergence of built environments in the evolution of the human line is the result less (or secondarily) of an aggrandizement of one or another primate behavioral trait and more (or primarily) the result of a coordination, coalescence, and transformative reordering of a nexus of significative behaviors in a variety of modalities. Architectonic evolution necessarily implicates all other developmental processes in every modality, and the emergence of any one sign-system in human culture is unthinkable without the emergence of every other.

In order to understand this multidimensional and multimodal evolution—both holistically and in its unimodal detail—it is necessary to address a number of important questions. For example, is it reasonable to postulate a gradual evolution or a singular set of inventions or conceptual breakthroughs close together in time? What *kind* of evidence would be required to confidently assert one or the other model? Are the family resemblances between our own architectonic codes and the earliest fossil traces of settlement structure greater than their differences? Are such differences as may be evidenced of a fundamental rather than a superficial nature? Can we in fact point to a particular time period or place wherein we can say with some confidence that the patterns of settlement organization are significantly different from earlier (and/or nonhuman) patterns of environmental appropriation and structuration? Is there evidence in the fossil record to suggest a gradual change over many millennia?

The tentative conclusions suggested by the present inquiry would clearly be strengthened were we to possess less ambiguous archaeological evidence. What evidence we do have is highly tantalizing and suggestive, and on its own grounds is open to the most varied interpretation.

In order to address the issues of interest to our inquiry, we shall have to bring to bear on these questions a great deal of indirect and implicational evidence, including not only the nature of latter-day (i.e. post-Paleolithic) architectonic organization, but also a comparative understanding of human and nonhuman communicational systems (zoosemiotics),[2] and also a comparative understanding of 'animal architecture' (zooarchitectonics), including the entire range of space and place-making activities among primates in general (display, gesture, territoriality). In short, we must understand any complex of activities and behavioral traits (such as toolmaking and use or time-telling) which contribute to the conceptual and artifactual transmutation of an environment.

This implies a theoretical and analytic undertaking which is beyond the scope not only of any one analytic study, but in particular of the present essay. In order to address these issues in a productive manner it will be necessary to establish a collaborative coordination of many different points of view and analytic methodologies. The result, if it is to be at all productive, must eschew a reductionism of approach in favor of a cluster of theories which synechdochally address overlapping portions of this nexus of problems.

The present study aims at the elaboration of one such synechdochal perspective, focussed upon the generic issue of human semiotic origins and evolution from the standpoint of the built environment. We must remain absolutely clear in the present undertaking that the picture of the origins and development of human semiosis elaborated from an architectonic perspective will necessarily be incomplete, open-ended, and inexorably subject to transformation and obsolescence over time, in precisely the same sense that a picture of human semiosis from a linguistic perspective is itself incomplete. Nor will it be the case that a holistic overview of human semiosis and its origins shall comprise a simple sum of atomistic perspectives: every discovery in any semiotic area bears implications for all others.

One of the most important reasons for the elaboration of an architectonic perspective on human semiosis and its origins is that direct evidence for architectonic behavior carries our view back at least a third of a million years, whereas direct linguistic records only appear at the earliest some ten millennia ago.[3] The student of built environments, then, is in a (relatively) privileged position with respect to an understanding of semiotic evolution in the human line.

But the accidents of the fossil evidence should not be taken as indicative of some genaeological primacy of the emergence of the architectonic system. Indeed, the cognitive sophistication manifested (as we shall argue below) in the settlement station at Terra

Amata in France of 300,000 years B.P. would be remarkably bizarre without a corresponding advance in other modalities.[4]

It is clear that the question of the origins of the architectonic code is inexorably bound up with an understanding of its functional and formal organization. It is necessary in the first place to understand what the built environment as we know it accomplishes which was not accomplished prior to its appearance, or accomplished in deeply divergent ways. It will be argued below that it is only through a revelation of the system's semiotic organization that we can approach this and other phylogenetic questions in a nontrivial fashion.

Profoundly implicated in such an inquiry is the question of the relationship between built artifacts and visual perception. We need to know if there are significant differences in the perceptual address and processing of architectonic and artifactual information as opposed to nonarchitectonic or nonartifactual visual information. Do artifactual formations provide users with a perceptual 'gain' over perceived portions of nonarchitectonic arrays? In what ways do built forms *mark* the presence of human individuals and groups, and how do made environments serve as data-banks for sociocultural information?

Considered in a holistic sense, the built environment is the instrumentality *par excellence* of the set of activities constituting the 'tool kit' of our species, and in a sense comprises the apotheosis of primate toolmaking. Its medium is coterminous, materially, with the entire set of perceptually palpable resources of the planetary biosphere (including our own and other bodies). But each architectonic code, from a material point of view, appropriates given landscape resources in particular microecologies. As a system, it is deeply semiautonomous with respect to given materials, in evident contrast to the architectonic environments of other species.

At base, in other words, the built environment is a *system of relationships* among *signs* (*not* among forms or materials *per se*). Hence, whereas its media may appear various and abruptly divergent (from a constrained perspective), in fact its medium is uniform, comprising motor-optically palpable formation *per se*. This does not mean, however, that an architectonic code merely appropriates material formation which somehow exists in an aprioristic manner, to be abstractly 'tagged' or conceptually labelled; an architectonic system is a system of *signs*, comprised of copresent *signantia* and *signata*. Conversely, there are no aprioristically existent conceptual domains which are simply manifested in available material formation. Whatever may be panhuman or universal in, e.g. the concept of dwelling, is necessarily *always* manifest within the conventional parameters of specific codes, however temporarily useful it may be, for analytic or other purposes, to reify such *signata*.

Because it is a semiotic system of a particular type, there exists in the architectonic code a dynamic and systemically functional balance between sign types of a sense-determinative nature and a sense-discriminative nature. Tendencies toward the invariant association of given *signata* with given *signantia* are invariably balanced by a diachronic and diatopic semiautonomy of connection. This rather vexed nature of architectonic 'symbolism' will be addressed at some length below.[5]

Human built environments are subject to change and transformation over space and time—a characteristic not demonstrated for the architectonic environments of other species; this property is itself a manifestation of the fact that the code is fundamentally a system of relationships rather than a system of forms. In nonhuman spheres, it appears to be generally the case that such variation is approximately coterminous with somatic and morphological radiation. In the human line, individuals who live in glass houses are not transparent. The great strides made in recent years in the area of zoosemiotics have served to highlight not only the equivalencies but also the abrupt differences in the organizational properties of architectonic environments in the human and nonhuman spheres. One of the purposes of the present volume is to seek a clarification of such equivalencies and differences from an architectonic perspective.

One salient property of architectonic systems, which has profound implications for our understanding of architectonic semiosis, is its *spatiotemporality*. Built environments are not meant to be read or used as passive stage sets or two-dimensional backdrops. The significative organization of a built environment is as temporal as it is spatial: settlements are designed to be construed spatially over time. In contrast to the unilinear temporality of speech-acts (which decay instantaneously), environmental constructs are four-dimensionally syntagmatic arrays, and manifest, moreover, a (relative) object-permanence. One of the patent implications of this fact is that, whatever may be shared between linguistic and architectonic systems in terms of semiotic design, they cannot be compared *directly*: their organizations are (as we shall see below) systemically *correlative* rather than parallel. A building is not simply a particularly clever way of writing texts in three dimensions, any more than verbal language is merely architecture in Flatland. And despite their overlapping correlativities of function, they are not simply two different ways of doing the 'same' things.

The format of the present inquiry comprises a temporally synechdochic focus upon a number of factors which it is felt need to be addressed in a consideration of architectonic (and semiotic) origins and evolution. Its organization, then, is necessarily cumulative. We shall begin, in Chapter II, with an examination of tool use, object manipulation and spatial behavior in the primate sphere. Chapters III and IV comprise a discussion of the nature of the functional and formative organization of built environments as we presently know them, while Chapter V consists of an essay on architectonic development and evolution in the light of the implications of the previous chapters. Chapter VI outlines some of the implications of this inquiry for a semiotic theory of culture *per se*, and Chapter VII is a summary discussion of the entire study, highlighting its firmer and weaker assertions.

NOTES

1. In particular we may note the work of Ulric Neisser (1976) and J. Hochberg (1978).
2. See especially in this regard the work of T. A. Sebeok, as introduced in 'Animal communication' (1965:1006-1014) and continued in 'Discussion of communication processes' (1967); *Animal Communication: Techniques of Study and Results of Research* (1968); *Perspectives in Zoosemiotics* (1972). See also S. B. Petrovich and E. H. Hess (1978:17-53) with extensive bibliography.
3. See D. Schmandt-Besserat (1977, 1978).
4. Excavations at Terra Amata (Nice) conducted and reported by H. de Lumley (1966, 1969), C. O. Sauer (1962), W. A. Fairservis (1975, *passim*) and R. Leakey and R. Lewin (1978:175 ff.).
5. See below, Chapter IV, and Note 9.

2

Tool Use, Object Manipulation, and Spatial Behavior

BACKGROUND

Homo sapiens is not the only species to use tools or to physically modify and alter its environment to enhance its chances of survival *vis-a-vis* geographically coterminous and competitive species: indeed, many different species exhibit these traits, from the simplest microorganisms which chemically alter their ambient surroundings to the social insects who erect technologically complex structures (see Alcock 1972; Lancaster 1968; van Lawick-Goodall 1971; von Frisch 1974; Wilson 1975).

In most instances, tool use *per se* is associated directly with food gathering, as in the case where an ant-lion (*Neuroptera*) will shower sand particles on prey walking by or at the top of a small sand pit constructed by a larva residing at the bottom, the particles being propelled by the head with the effect of knocking prey into the bottom of the pit-trap (Alcock 1972:465).

The use and manufacture of tools, however, is nowhere more intense and prevalent than among the primates, and, among primates, humans appear to be unique in the extent to which they rely upon the instrumental manipulation of their environments in daily life. Particularly widespread in the human line is the trait of using tools to make tools—in other words, the making of objects whose function is to construct other objects. This is manifest throughout the human behavioral repertoire, and occurs everywhere in culture.

In language, for example, the set of sign-types includes certain signs whose chief function is to build and contrast directly-significative components (morphemes, words). These signs (phonemes) are devoid of significance in themselves,[1] and their primary meaning is systemic. Similarly, the architectonic system includes certain sign-formations (*forms*)[2] which serve principally to distinguish other sign-formations (*cells,* cell *matrices*) which are themselves meaningful in contrastive opposition to ther such constructs. Thus a 'wall', as a *form*, is meaningful insofar as it serves to define and delimit a given space-*cell* in opposition to other *cells*.

This is not to say, however, that a given *form* may not in addition carry a direct significance in terms of its sensory articulation. In such a case (as where rectilinear *forms* signify the presence of a given social class in contrast to curvilinear ones which signify other associations), the 'wall' as a *form*, a geometric entity, carries a double function (systemic as well as significative), but its primary function is systemic. Similar processes are apparent in linguistic codes.[3]

This is above and beyond a given *form*'s material articulation or realization, which may be similarly multifunctional as an element in the definition of a geometric unity as well as being directly significative (as where the use of limestone may be associated with a given social class in a given culture, in contrastive social status). In this sense, a brick may be seen as a tool to make a toolmaking tool.

Let us look at the background of human tool use and manufacture among our primate cousins. The order of primates is perhaps some seventy million years old, and reached its greatest diversity, proliferation, and geographical expansion some fifty to sixty million years ago. After that time, primates became relatively insignificant as an order until about twelve millennia ago when one of its species, *homo sapiens*, domesticated plants and animals and began a geographical radiation which was soon to cover many of the habitable ecological niches of the planet.

But the human line, including such ancestors as *homo erectus* and *Australopithecus*, may have diverged from the primate line of apes as early as ten million years ago. At any rate, the earliest known tools made by individuals in the human line appear about three million years ago, and remained largely unchanged morphologically until about one million years B.P. The basic tool kit prior to this time consisted of stones of rounded configuration, used apparently for bashing; crudely trimmed flakes employed as knives and scrapers; and rough stones used for chopping. During this period of two million years there was no evident change in the techniques of toolmaking; there was no apparent standardization in toolmaking techniques, and no regional specialization of tool kits.

About a million years ago there appears to have begun a rapid evolution of brain size and complexity of tool assemblages, associated with the emergence of a single species of tool user, *homo erectus*, who soon came to dominate much of the Old World. It seems that the skill and efficiency in the use of tools by this group is associable with their geographic success, and may have resulted in a concomitant decline in the number of primate species in competition for the same environments.

An intriguing artifact of this period is a stone circle uncovered at Olduvai by Leakey, of unknown function but suggesting a built emplacement or locus of activity of some kind.[4] Consisting of a single line of stones forming the circumference of what would have been a circle of about ten feet in diameter, this object stands apparently alone as the earliest environmental artifact in the faint record of the early human line. It is not known whether the circle of stones served to ground and support upright objects such as twigs and branches which might have served to delimit a walled (or possibly roofed) enclosure, in the fashion of the structures at Terra Amata some two-thirds of a million years later in southern France,[5] which we shall discuss below.

Many nonprimates use tools, but there is apparently a significant difference between the tool-using behaviors of primates and those of other animal groups: no nonprimate uses such *different* objects in manipulating the environment. Other tool-using species tend to use only one kind of tool per species, and more often than not such tool use is patterned in highly evolved and stereotypic sequences of movement. Moreover, many such 'tools' are in fact evolved instrumental appendages of the body itself—claws, teeth, beaks, etc.

In the primate order we observe more of a generalized tendency to manipulate objects and to use them in differing kinds of situations.

There is also a major difference between the universal and constant use of tools by humans and the comparatively rare and incidental use of tools by (for example) the chimpanzee, for whom tool use is a relatively small part of the behavioral complex. The same contrast is evident with our own ancestral *homo erectus* and *Australopithecus*. The human being is completely immersed in a behavioral complex which is dominated by instrumental alterations of the environment and of other human beings. Moreover, the human 'tool kit' characteristically enlarges over time, and this repertory is constantly changing with respect to the subtlety, complexity, and focussing power of its components. Both highly specific and greatly generalized, multifunctional tools coexist, and the ranges of their usefulness are in continual expansion or contraction.

Chimpanzees, like humans, learn to make and use tools by social imitation and learning. They use tools in two kinds of contexts—when feeding or carrying out some other nonemotional activity (Lancaster 1975:51 ff.), and in the context of excited, aggressive display.

Chimps are known to employ found sticks or twigs as probes for extracting termites from nests, or when feeding on ants or dipping for honey in bee's nests. Sticks are also used as levers for prying open recalcitrant objects, and stones are employed to crack open hard-shelled fruits or nuts. In addition, a chimpanzee will use handfuls of partly-chewed leaves as sponges for dipping water out of crevices too small for a whole face to enter, as well as for wiping water or dirt from the body itself.

They also use anything that comes to hand in defense and aggressive display: often objects are thrown about at random in excitement. But it appears to be the case that such objects are not used in actual fighting, and they are evidently not aimed at an enemy: attack is normally made with hands and teeth. Objects are not, then, used as weapons but rather as random components in agonistic display for the purpose of intimidating others, accompanied by loud and aggressive vocalizations.

The tool-using chimpanzee suggests the *kind* of ape ancestor which might be postulated for the background to the emergence of the human line—*viz*. an ape that used tools for a variety of different reasons, in various ways, and in concert with other activities. It may well have been the accumulated influence of many ways of (and reasons for) using tools and manipulating objects which might have taken selective pressure off the specific situation, tool, and movement; natural selection might then have acted upon a broader category of behavior, for example one involving the co-ordination of brain, hand, eye, and objects in general, in the context of a wide variety of social and ecological situations and problems.

The question of tool use is significant to our inquiry for a variety of reasons, most notably with respect to its relationship to *environmental reference*. Tool use in itself focusses optical and motor attention upon objects and fine details of an environment, and in effect channels and orients the perception of palpable distinctive contrasts in an environment.

It is a significant step from environmental reference and its focussed marking through the use of appropriated objects to environmental *structuration* and ordering wherein assemblages of objects of various types are employed not only as instruments but also self-consciously as sign-complexes habitually and conventionally associated with aspects of social behavior.

Tool using and making is evidently an important selective midwife to the ability to form associations between an abstract concept and a tangible object, which in turn is itself a necessary precondition to the evolution of language and built environments. It is of interest in this regard to consider that the communicative systems of nonhuman primates also do appear to make patent reference to the environment—e.g. in cases wherein the latter is employed as an accomplice in the expression of emotive information about individuals. Human language, on the other hand, while also communicating information about the emotional state of speaker and/or addressee, gives finely detailed referential information about social relationships and the phsyical environment, *in addition to* information about the communicating channel itself.

This is not to assert, however, that emotional reference *per se* is necessarily in any way more 'primitive' than object-reference. Rather, each involves different kinds of *referential orientation*. Furthermore, it is not necessary to assert that emotionally expressive language must be a substratum with regard to other expressive and communicative functions: every language has its own corpus-specific ways to say 'ouch'!

For early (and contemporary) human foragers, the ability to

make finely-discriminative environmental reference would be adaptively important, particularly among groups which are dependent for their food upon gathering and hunting over broad areas of an ecological niche. The efficient utilization of the resources of a territory would have been greatly enhanced, moreover, if members of a foraging party could split up into subgroups, rejoining after a day or week.

But, as J. B. Lancaster rightly notes (Lancaster 1975:73), this capability presupposes some sort of spatiotemporal denotation realizable as a *place* to meet, consult, compare notes, share food, and plan the next foray (Lancaster 1975:74). Such a home base or general headquarters might be more or less permanent (though this might limit the effective foraging range), or seasonally or periodically recurrent; it may be a previously designated meeting camp somewhere within the territory of the group.

At any rate, the linkage of a vocal label with such an environmental marking-distinction (however materially articulated) would have provided, we may imagine, an enhanced and partly redundant way to designate such spatiotemporal coordinates. As Lancaster notes:

The ability for environmental reference both reflects and permits a relationship between the species and its environment different from that of other primates. The emergence of language was related to changes in the ecology of the evolving hominid species. According to this view, the evolution of the abilities to use tools and to name are closely linked (Lancaster 1975:74).

One of the characteristic properties of human language as currently known is its perceptual enhancement or redundancy. A given message or speech-act more often than not carries with it redundant information regarding the nature and orientation of its component referents. This redundancy serves to strengthen the transmission of a message within unpredictably noisy contexts, so that if for whatever reason a portion of the transmission is erased, the sense of the totality will be largely reconstructible with the remainder. Of course some lexical formations are necessarily more crucial to decoding than others, and what will be more or less redundant is a function of language-specific rules of formation and patterning.

Communicative redundancy, moreover, is achievable not only through channel-strengthening strategies, but is also realizable *multimodally*. Thus, gesture or other forms of somatic signing, while themselves often semiautonomous of language systems, additionally tend to be culture-specific,[6] and may serve to augment a speech-act in the transmission of information: the speaker will be saying the 'same' (or contextually equivalent) thing with two 'vocabularies', so to speak. If the addressee misses a given name, the identity may be supplied by the orientation of a finger toward the referent. The important point here is that verbal language is *characteristically* embedded in multimodal communicative complexes in daily behavior, and it is simultaneously capable of being analyzed out as a single channel where necessary, under appropriate conditions,[7] for example in the dark or where the body or environment is invisible, or perceptually obscured.

In our view no single evolutionary advance would have had significant value without the rest of some such multimodal or rebus-like pattern (tools, gathering and hunting, bipedalism, naming, etc.), and no single component can be entirely understood alone: each consists of an interactive component of a broad adaptive complex of behaviors. In this regard, a system such as vocal language should—at least to judge from the nature of current language systems—have been multifunctional *in its origins*, concerned not only with environmental naming or labeling, but also with the communication of emotional self-reference, with the maintenance of phatic contact, with conative assertion, and so forth.[8]

We would also stress a similar and/or concomitant multifunctionality with respect to environmental appropriation and object-construction, and suggest that built environments are equivalently multifunctional and multiply referential, and are similarly characteristically embedded in multimodal activity. As we shall see below, it is evidently the case that the various semiotic systems comprising human culture are designed (and, we shall suggest, designed from the outset) to operate *both* singly and in multimodal, deictically-integrated ways.

In addition to toolmaking activity and object manipulation, the complex of environmental and social ordering strategies generally subsumed under the heading 'territoriality' is often alluded to as providing one of the important background components of the emergence of the built environment. The next section will be concerned with this set of issues and its relationship to the organization and emergence of built environments.

TERRITORIALITY

By 'territoriality' here will be meant the variety of means whereby the dispersal of individuals in a population, and of that population as a whole, is spatiotemporally ordered—the mapping, so to speak, of a social group and its members onto a landscape. This deployment or mapping does not consist, among social groups of primates, of individuals of equal status or function, but rather comprises the mapping of a socially structured network or lattice of individuals with characteristic types of interpersonal orientations of attention and address (Lancaster 1975:44 ff.).

It is generally surmised that the early hominids were nonarboreal primates that had invaded ecological niches comparable to those of predatory carnivores, and that they had become over time modified in a variety of ways for efficient life in such niches. Their geographical ranges would have been considerably more extensive than those of other living primates, and they would have had to adapt to such ranges with certain kinds of sensory equipment, initially less effective than those of other resident mammals. The olfactory labels, for example, with which social animals such as wolves mark a territory and map a perceptual world would not have been available to the hominids.

The problem of developing adequate labels to mark a social range may have required the enhancement of visual, auditory, and vocal capacities. The lattice of interpersonal cohesions could have been enhanced and strengthened through the elaboration of auxiliary modalities such as conventionalized vocalization which not only served to signal the relative emotional states of individuals but which also had the power to finely discriminate different souces of information in the environment. Such a modality would face the problem of transmitting perceptual cues regarding the

similarities and differences among percepts, as well as the gradations of similarity among classes of percepts taken as homologous,
involving, in the latter case, some kind of schemata of modification.

Evolved verbal language such as we know it operates as a stream
of vocalizations over time wherein relationships are transmuted
into patterned sequences of signs of various types purporting to
simulate such relationships. Speech-acts comprise syntactic or
syntagmatic arrangements of signs whose relative arrangement,
specified by the particular rules of formation specific to a given
language, simulate interrelationships (among any set of events or
objects) which may not necessarily be similarly sequential—e.g.
paradigmatic, or syntagmatically simultaneous (bundled), embedded, and multidimensional relationships.

Verbal language does this in particularly clever ways, employing
systems of minute contrastive oppositions among sounds which
have no direct significance, but which serve to contrast larger units
of sound-sequences from each other, thereby providing ordered
sets of signs with ranges of meaningful associations specific to a
group.

Such a system did not evolve in a vacuum and can only have
emerged within the context of the emergence of a variety of sign-
systems addressing partly similar problems in different modalities.
In particular, for a variety of reasons to be discussed below, the
evolution of verbal languages and built environments cannot be
atomistically disambiguated, and it is evident that both developments in some way went closely in hand, in a mutually interactive manner. In a number of interesting respects, the functional
and formative organization of each system is built upon and implies the other.

It would undoubtedly be adaptive if information received from
different sense modalities could be given a *common code* or model,
yielding a perceptual world in which various kinds of sensory information about objects and events in space and time. In the case
of early hominids, verbal language which incorporated or encoded
finely detailed environmental information would provide one portion of a solution to the problem of creating a real world which
was a useful simulative model of sensory events.

We would suggest that in concert with the latter there arose a complementary, reinforcing and partly parallel solution wherein the humanly important structure of a territory could be encoded by means of visually palpable cues or markings which would serve to transmit behavioral information.

A territory or foraging range comprises a landscape whose components are not of equal weight or value with respect to their usefulness as food resources: there will exist for any social group a complex set of informational cues of varying importance for survival. In addition, not all such information would have been equally important to each social group.

We would expect that a given group would employ any conceivable means for expressing and communicating to its members the relative importance for survival of the resources of an environment. Some food sources will be found to be edible, and others poisonous; some will be of greater nutritional value than others. It is crucial for a parent to know if the berries or fruits in the reach of a child are poisonous or not, and the survival of that child will depend upon the ability of a parent to effectively communicate such information. The development of efficient physical and vocal constraints upon behavior would provide a way of insuring such survival, to a certain degree.

In short, members of a group must build themselves into a structure of behavior whose systemic and componential gradation itself serves to *track experience* in such a way as to maximize the efficient exploitation of environmental resources while minimizing danger to life and limb.

The environment or territory itself must be perceptually ordered so as to provide communicative cues as to its varying dangers and delights; it must be modelled, in effect, so as to speak for itself as to what it offers the individual and group. The individual, when out alone, must remember how to *read* the environment in the ways taught by his fellows or parent(s) so that he may return alive.

He must remember a great many things, from information about the inedibility of green berries to the significant differences between these and a tiger's tracks. He must know that when a flock of birds suddenly rises to the air in the distance there is potential danger approaching, and he must know how to finely discriminate the noises made by squirrels or snakes in the shrubbery.

In effect, he must employ his sight and his hearing, and indeed all of his senses, to survive; and he must be capable of testing hypotheses with anything available: if two sets of tracks are deceptively similar formally, he must look for other signs to distinguish a safe animal from a predatory one. The two animals may sound very different, or smell different, or the carcasses of the characteristic prey of the one will differ from the remains of the chewed branches of the other.

Everything, in other words, must be significant in some way; he cannot assume that some things are mute. He must treat his environment as a being-which-speaks in multiple ways and for different reasons. Every perceptually palpable distinction in the environment, every edge and surface, must be treated as symptomatic evidence, as an index or as a 'sign'.

This is not to say that everything will be equally meaningful; on the contrary, all the bits of information will be *ordered relative to each other*.

One of the tasks facing the individual is that of resolving perceptual ambiguity. In the case of deceptively similar tracks, form /A/ can be distinguished from form /A'/ through the habitual concatenative association of either with another formation which more patently distinguishes the two: /A/ + /x/ vs. /A'/ + /y/. The nature of such syntagmatic modification will necessarily vary according to the signing medium. In some media, modification may occur in a simultaneous, embedded or superimposed fashion rather than sequentially, or by the replacement of two ambiguous signs by two contrastive formations (i.e. /A/ vs. /B/ instead of /A/ + /x/ or /y/).

One of the evident results of habitual concatenative modification may have been a concomitant deemphasis on the significative value of the *individual* sign and an enhancement of the value of sign-*patterns*.

In other words, we may expect the concurrent emergence of sign-complexes whose component formations become indirectly or systemically significant. At any rate, whatever the processes involved,[9] such a process might suggest the development of an internally-ordered system of signs—for example, vocalizations—wherein palpably-contrastive auditory elements become systemic instrumentalities in the definition of larger formations of direct signification: in other words, sounds to build words, or tools to make tools.

Visual and verbal media may employ both syntagmatic contrasts and paradigmatic oppositions, but they will differ markedly with respect to their relative abilities to efficiently encode such relationships. For example, it has been suggested[10] that verbal language is relatively limited with regard to its capacity to clearly and 'iconically' embed percepts within each other, which is apparently a function of the constraints of temporal-auditory memory. By contrast, visual formations allow greater complexity of infixing.

At any rate, there will be evident advantages to a capacity to portray finely discriminated information in different ways and for different purposes. It may be more immediately informative, for example, to indicate the vulnerable portions of a food animal through iconically diagrammatic means than by linguistic circumlocution. On the other hand, this is a function of purpose, and there are evident advantages to the ability to encode and transmit information in different ways, and under variable contextual conditions: it may be better to communicate information silently, through diagrammatic gesture, when any vocal noise might trigger a flight reaction in a prey in close proximity.

If it is taken as a reasonable assumption that the social life of early hominids was not profoundly different from that observable among our extant primate cousins such as the chimpanzees, then the fact that the hominid child was born into a complex and finely graded social order may provide us with a background or substratum 'matrix of relationships'—an ordered system—which would have offered a useful model for the general ordering of perceptual experience.

For the individual in an advanced primate society to function effectively, he must continually assess the complex behaviors of his fellows so as to provide effective bases for his own behavior. Such behavior will depend upon the efficient perception and translation of multimodal activity wherein information arriving more or less simultaneously in a number of sense modalities is habitually concatenated and patterned in ordered displays or gestalts. He will characteristically attend to information which is multimodal and multifunctional. He will also characteristically analyze out such sensory information so that isolated sensory information—portions of a total gestalt—may synechdochally cue the remainder of the totality. A 'part' of a display or scene may trigger the memory of the 'whole'.

He will, in effect, be involved in operant behavior which reveals perceptual redundancies of information, and he must be able to read the signs of some impending behavior on the part of another so as to react quickly and effectively. He must learn to read the initial warning signs of another's anger, for example, or the beginning indices of invitation.

Furthermore, he will have to learn routines of habitual orientation and address to his fellows—in other words, the spatial geometry of behavior which serves as a system of ordered cues to social structure. He does not live in a homogeneous field of social interaction, and social space itself is highly charged and systematized by means of contrastive relative orientations associated with different kinds of interpersonal relationships. He will learn that the relative orientations of two bodies carries cues as to the momentary and/or invariant social positions of those individuals, and he will know that two individuals are grooming or mating, sharing food or confronting each other. Furthermore, he will learn who grooms whom at what times and for how long, who dominates whom with respect to the order of mating with a female in estrus, and so forth.

He is made conscious at every moment that his identity is defined and built into a complexly-ordered social environment, the *topology* of whose internal relationships may remain more or less invariant under positional location and movement. In effect, the individual must be conceptually sophisticated enough to apprehend the *relational invariance* inherent to all aspects of collective life—the fact, in other words, that two events or formations may be partly the same and partly different.

The organizational logic of semiotic systems as we know them would have required for their emergence some model of relationships of multiple kinds which was in some sense already given. It may be suggested that the geometry of social ordering itself could have served as such a model for (what might have involved) the abstraction-and-simulation of its features in order to provide enhanced, semiautonomous systems of representation and communication. We may speculate that the emergence of semiotic systems such as verbal languages and built environments represents, at least in part, the transformative reification of such ordered relationships, and the effective encoding of many kinds of relationships from a variety of perspectives within the constraints offered by different signaling media. The occasion for such a process, we may imagine, may have been related to an increased capacity to attend to portions of a gestalt—for example the impending, oncoming cues of an imminent display (of any type)—so that such component signals are taken as evidential indices, to serve as signs in their own right in a semidetachable fashion. Such a capacity to read warning signals without having to process the whole of a behavioral display is common to many species (as a dog will come to know that putting on one's shoes is a signal that she is to be taken for a walk, or that a vocalization of a certain type may be an equivalent sign).

Clearly, we are not claiming that the organization of a sign-system is a direct transitive reflection of the organization of social structure itself. Rather, we are suggesting that *the geometries of relationship* exhibited by social structure may have provided a conceptual model, or set of resources, for transformative simulation. In this sense, we must look to underlying correlativities and equivalencies of organization, to features of formative process held in common.

Physical marking and vocal labeling must have been apprehended as redundant to a certain degree in early human societies. An individual may indicate an environmental distinction to others through the utterance of a distinctive configuration of sound waves which contrast with other configurations recalled as being associated with contrastive environmental percepts. He may also indicate the same object or event with a variety of other means— by somatic signing or by producing an artifact which, like the vocal sign, serves to simulate an association in a conventionally understood fashion (i.e. as a formation which depends for its understanding on a formative *contrast* with other signs).

It has been observed that human neonates habitually and characteristically associate vocal labels with visual percepts such that the former is construed as one of a set of properties inherent to an object or event.[11] Children appear to be innately disposed toward the creation of such multimodal assemblages and the apprehension of multimodal gestalts, and are involved practically from birth in the processes of coordinating information taken from more than one sensory channel.[12] Early models of objects and events would appear to resemble complexly-ordered rebuses within which visual and verbal features are particularly closely linked. It is evidently the case that phylogenetic development is involved with ongoing dynamic syntheses of information along with concurrent analyses of component features of synthetic constructs into increasingly ordered channel-specific modules of information. The child is continually assessing the partial similarity and partial difference among objects, events and situations, and the invariance and variability of experiences and their transformations.

Whether semiotic ontogenesis mirrors neonate phylogeny or not, it may be suggested that the process of emergence of each system as a semiautonomous or semidetachable code involved at least the abstraction and coordination of different kinds of information residing in different sense-modalities so as to give rise to a *cluster* or 'common codes' which could function broadly to represent variously-useful perspectives on experience.

It may be suggested, in other words, that verbal language, as a comprehensive and encyclopedic 'common code' for the representation and communication of salient information arose *as one of a set* of similarly effable 'common codes' which provided individuals with various intertranslatable ways to accomplish partly-equivalent things.

Because of the evident equivalent processes of formation among human semiotic systems, it would appear that evolved human culture itself came to serve as a matrix or ordered network of partly-redundant functional systems operating as channel-specific transforms of each other. As a superordinate system of ordered ensembles, a culture may be seen as an integrated set of transformed, intersecting and partially-overlapping stratagems for ordering existence. Rather than merely running in parallel, the set of ensembles would occupy partly-integrated, multidemsional lattices wherein changes induced in one figure induce concomitant recalibrations in one or more of the others. Intersystemic relationships would be held in equilibration by a dynamic synchrony (Bower 1977:30-32).

Information will be preserved differently in various codes, providing a multiply-stereoscopic perspective on objects and events. Not all information palpable in one code will be relevant or easily representable in another. Moreover, the functions of each code will not be coterminous, and within each code a message will itself display a variety of functional orientations, one or another being dominant at a given time.

In the broadest sense, the meaningfulness of a formation is a function of the geometry of intersemiotic transmutation (Jakobson 1971a:260-266, i.p.) or translative relationship (following Peirce) between one sign and another or others. A semiotic system is designed to interact with other systems, and each characteristically contains formative components whose meaning cannot be specified without particular orientations upon the referential (and cross-modal) context of a transmission. Our understanding of the processes of semiosis would be enhanced by a clearer picture of the mechanisms of *deixis* evident in all codes.

From the perspective of the formations and communicative signals of other species, human artifactual formations have a curiously 'blurred' identity. Whereas many nonprimates such as birds or fishes often respond to a single patch of color or bodily gesture (and virtually nothing else) (Lancaster 1975:12 f.), the primate *more consistently* responds to the appearance of an entire body in space, its postures and soundings, in the context of the history of previous encounters with that other individual. There is, as we have noted, a characteristic tendency to respond to information from more than one sense modality, and to manifest a simultaneous summation of complex sets of signals in interpersonal behavior.

Among primates, individual relations are personalized, finely graded, and rapidly changing, and there tends to be a premium put on the precise expression of mood. Because the primate lives in a complex social field in which it must respond to many individuals simultaneously, individual behavior is often *compromised* among a set of possible actions, each of which must be subtly weighed against the other. As recently noted (Chance and Jolly 1970:503-518) individual social fields are conceptualized in terms of 'attention structures': it is a crucial social fact for an individual to know whom to pay attention to at what time, and primates are continually assessing the flux of behavior of their fellows in order to establish bases for their own behavior. Attention may be unilinear and directed, as in the case of hierarchies of dominance, or synchronically reciprocal, as in a mother-child dyad.

Primates communicate their motivational states by means of complex displays which include physical posturing and/or movement and vocalizations. Such gestalts simultaneously incorporate various types and grades of information. The ability to predict social behaviors is crucial to the evolution of complex social systems, and it is in the context of such complex communicative behaviors that we may begin to understand the adaptive nature of environmental structuration, which functions as a component in sets of composite signals. Concomitantly, as an ordered system of signs itself, a built environment exhibits a variety of functions depending upon the relationship of its component entities to various aspects of its relational context; in this regard, a comparison may be made with the language code, as we shall discuss below in Chapter III.

It may be suggested, then, that there came to exist a series of homologous relationships between the organization of a code and of its component relations with other communicative signals in composite modalities, and that the 'design template' for such an organization may have been provided in part by social structure itself.

In this sense, a culture may be seen as providing a conceptual framework, a parallel world which can be employed to measure variation and register cohesions. In order for such a complexly-integrated modality to function reasonably well in a changing and dynamic social field, it would have had to have been modeled in some fashion on the peculiarly flexible and multivalent organization of social structure itself.

We are principally interested here in the role of built environments in this evolutionary process. It should be clear by now that the architectonic system cannot simply be a direct translation of animal (and especially primate) 'territoriality'. In the human line, 'territoriality' has become essentially a *component* function in a broader systemic organization.

In other words, the territorial role of built environments coexists with a variety of architectonic functions, and, by being assimilated to the latter as a code, it is thereby changed in its nature. Not only does a built environment map and frame the topological boundaries of the territory of a social group, it also encodes and communicates group-specific pathways and recursive routines and interpersonal orientations characteristic of that group.

An architectonic system appropriates and incorporates machines, vehicles, natural formations—indeed anything and everything visually palpable, including individuals. A tree and a machine do not cease to be what they are when so appropriated; rather, they are absorbed into a system of relationships, becoming significative nodes in a relational network. In short, they become *signs*, often of a highly complex and composite nature. While it may be useful for certain purposes to distinguish an 'appropriated' tree next to which a dwelling is constructed from one which is deliberately grown to delimit and order an ambient landscape, in both cases the tree becomes a component sign in an architectonic *system*. Furthermore, that tree or stand of trees need not be related to its built relatives in a formal geometric fashion for it to function architectonically; the gardens of Versailles are no more 'architectonically' organized than the appropriated ambient surroundings of an English country manor house.

An architectonic code is built upon subsets of contrastive formative features which serve in a corpus-specific fashion to create a 'vocabulary' and 'grammar' of objects (whether made or appropriated) which conventionally signify ordered sets of cognitive or somantic domains.

The constraints upon the selection and systemic incorporation of architectonic formations are very broad indeed, as even the most cursory cross-cultural examination of built environments will reveal. In short, an architectonic system comprises any and all of the spatially-palpable formations which humans may devise, construct, or appropriate from the environment in order to transmit information regarding the conceptual world of a society. This information, moreover, incorporates a variety of functions manifested as conventionally-understood orientations upon one or another of the component entities in a transmission—on the builder(s) themselves, on the historical context of prior constructs, on the symbolic content of the referent transmission, or, indeed, upon the construct itself in a self-conscious manner. An architectonic object may present a summation of the cosmic wisdom of a people as a simulative model of that group's ideal world (Borobudur; Chartres), to be read out *as* a multidimensional and multimodal 'text', or it may merely serve to highlight or call attention to a delimited transition point between two semantic domains (as with a city gate). In each case, however, a variety of orientations upon meaning will be found to inhere to that formation: even the most 'uncomplicated' architectonic object carries information about a wide variety of themes deemed significant by a society.[13]

At the same time that an architectonic formation may stage activity representing a relatively discrete semantic domain, it will simultaneously imply a set of domains within which the former achieves definition. Furthermore, two 'identical' formations in a setting may prescribe highly contrastive relationships with that setting: in an architectonic system, 'synonymy' seldom applies, and architectonic formations are inherently polysemous in corpus-specific ways.

Apparently identical formations in different corpora necessarily encode contrastive portions of the semantic universes of societies, since the meaningfulness of a formation will be the sum of the ordered sets of relationships which a formation enters into. This network or lattice of associations, moreover, exhibits a multifold existence wherein a set of conventionally prescribed associations overlaps with idiosyncratic domains modeled by different individuals. There exists a balance between invariance and contextual variation.

The conventional nature of architectonic signs—*viz.* the fact that architectonic systems of different societies constitute different systems which are partly opaque with respect to each other—

may have had multiple adaptive advantages in early human development. Conventionality or arbitrariness of reference (i.e. the fact that the meaningfulness of a formation is a function of culture-specific networks of association) is as much an artifact of the differing existential-ecological worlds of different human groups as it is a concomitant of deliberate group identity and self-definition. Different corpora or architectonic systems manifest a property of camouflage or relative opacity with respect to each other. What looks like a random stick in the ground to an outsider may be, to the insider, the sacred gnomon or *axis mundi* of his settlement.

Consider that one of the important problems facing an early human society will have been to preserve its range of territorial resources *vis-à-vis* the territories of other groups. Such a problem will have had many possible resolutions, many equivalent and redundant strategies. One such effective strategem may have been the use of the environment or territory itself to signify and cue the presence of a group.

The problem would be compounded by the evident fact that such territorial ranges would be relatively motile and shifting according to seasonally-available resources. Moreover, characteristic food-sources will prescribe differing routines of interaction: the territory of a group which depends for its subsistence upon the tracking of migratory reindeer will be notably different than that of a group dependent for its subsistence on the ecological relationships among small mammals, occasional large prey, and various vegetable foods.

At any rate, even in situations of only relatively stable territoriality, we may imagine that there evolved a variety of strategems for the effective marking of a range only seasonally or cyclically exploited. As we have noted above, the problems of survival call forth a variety of means for environmental marking and reference.

In this regard, an environmental 'mark' which in some way remains in a territory in the momentary or seasonal absence of a group will be required. In the visual channel, we may suppose that early humans came to rely on perceptible marks or traces which would endure to broadcast relevant information—enhanced objects of any type (comprising, minimally, some easily readable land-scape distinction in formation). The most general function of an enhanced environmental trace would be to signify a node in a net-work of behavioral associations. In this sense, there is a general equivalency between such formations as an arrow marked on a tree, a radio transmitter set up at the south pole, the cross planted by a conquistador in a new land, or a pile of stones left in a clear-ing.

A minimal requirement of such a mark is that its rate of decay be slower than the temporal patterns of return of a group or indi-vidual. It must continue to 'broadcast' relevant information on its own. (It may also be important that it do so without interference from the ecological niche itself, and it may have to manifest a cer-tain invisibility to outsiders—human or otherwise. It will coexist with a vast number of messages being transmitted by a wide var-iety of coterminous species, and it may have to coexist with trans-missions by other human groups. With regard to the latter, a con-ventionally agreed upon signal—e.g. a pile of stones rather than a bundle of sticks—will serve the dual role of advertisement and camouflage.)

Such an environmental mark is a human version of the chemical traces left by other species to signal territorial ownership, but will have a transmissional advantage over the latter in the sense that it will characteristically be constructed to outlast changes in weather conditions which may easily obliterate chemical signs. Once in place, it will broadcast continuously (unlike a verbal sign).

In line with what has been noted above, however, such marks or traces need not necessarily be strictly artifactual, but may comprise significant *appropriated* formations. There will be times when it is appropriate not to leave a made trace, when it may be advanta-geous to encode information about the spatial deployment of be-haviors through other channels, or in composite signals. The asso-ciation of a place (such as a distinctive stand of trees, or a conflu-ence of streams, or a high hill) with a verbal label may thus serve an equivalent function as the made trace (such as a ring of stones). In this case, the verbal sign will be copresent as a mentifact to be realized by the emergence of the environmental place (and/or its impending approach or pathway) into the visual channel.

The situation would most likely not have characteristically been so clear cut; as noisy, messy social mammals, a band of humans would inevitably leave semiotic droppings, metonymic marks and traces throughout its passage so that information is constantly being broadcast in all channels, subsuming dynamic, complex, composite signals of all kinds. As highly social primates, early humans would be constantly assessing not only the finely-graded behaviors of each other, but also the continual flux of environmental information. In short, everything must be treated as potential evidence for something; everything must be addressed with a question; everything has a story to tell: but it is equally necessary to know what to ignore as 'noise'.

Artifactual markings must satisfy requirements which seem, on the face of it, to be at cross-purposes. On the one hand, a mark must be sufficiently enhanced perceptually so as to be palpable to members of a group and to speak clearly to outsiders of passage and settlement claims. On the other hand, it should maintain sufficient opacity so as to be, to a certain extent, enigmatic: it may be necessary under certain conditions not to reveal too much about a group and its habits.

In effect, architectonic objects may need to balance properties of synechdochic *caricature* and *camouflage*. In the first place, certain salient properties of a given formation will require fewer perceptual samplings (e.g. saccadic eye-movements) to be recognizable more quickly and at greater distances. In the second place, it will require a greater number of perceptual samplings to be recognizable. A given object such as a hut may be very nearly 'invisible' to an outsider because it may employ for its material articulation edges, boundaries, and aggregations more like the random assemblages of environmental objects themselves. It will in some landscape-specific manner imitate the edges and boundaries of 'natural' formations. It will nevertheless jump out of the landscape just enough for an insider to recognize its meaning as a mark of habitation or encampment by his fellows. An architectonic system is addressed to the problem solving, illusion resolving, constructivist mechanisms of visual perception, and a building may 'lie' as effectively as a speech-act.

We in the societies spun off the European matrix, and some

others, often tend to equate architectonic objects with formations of regularized geometric configuration. A less narrow and parochial perspective will reveal that this is an accidental and corpus-specific property of architectonic materialization. The minimal require-ment for architectonic semiosis is (conventionalized) perceptually-palpable contrast to environmental setting, distinction within an ambient surround within the parameters specified by the needs of a given society. The reified contrast will serve as a node in a net-work of spatiotemporal oppositions to other formations so as to define portions of an ordered system of conceptual relationships.

A territory is transformed into an ordered system of architec-tonic relationships in a very wide variety of ways, as we have sug-gested, within the parameters of conventional and group-specific perceptibility. Necessarily, what (and how) we see is a complex function of societal organization and purpose.[14]

In this sense, it may be again asserted that a built environment serves at least in part as an *auxiliary sense-modality*, arrayed aside other artifactual and biological modalities so as to channel, stage, map, and direct activity of all kinds. A built environment is a model of the reality or realities of a society, staged in a spatio-temporal/geometric object-language which serves to cue the per-ception of culturally-important semantic domains through the ex-ploitation of characteristic patterns and processes of perceptual activity. Distinctions in formation are intended to signal differ-ences in meaning in precisely the same manner, but with very different means, as vocal language. As discussed elsewhere,[15] both codes are built upon distinctive formative features realized through complexly-integrated sets of binary (and in part n-ary) contrastive oppositions, within the constraints offered by dif-ferent media.

The fossil traces of environmental structuration by early humans are very faint indeed, and, furthermore, it has not been entirely clear what the student of architectonic origins should have been looking for. It does seem clear, however, that the environmental orderings of present-day less-economically-evolved societies pro-vide us with (albeit ambiguous) comparative evidence.

It may be of interest in this regard to note the observations of Jane Hill on the nature of place-naming among hunter-gatherer peoples (Hill 1974:185 ff.), where attention is called to the 'amazing proliferation' of place-names, a large number of one-sign expressions with highly specialized meanings. Hill suggests that this situation is in strong contrast to the place-naming habits of 'urban types' like ourselves, which characteristically involve complex expressions like 'six-sixty-six Lexington Avenue', or 'at the corner of Hollywood and Vine'.

It is not clear, however, whether such a contrast is in fact an artifact of specific language structures *per se*, and the question can not, as yet, be easily resolved. As Hill points out, we need to know a great deal more about a number of things, including other kinds of place-naming (and place-making) activities, particularly among extant children and adolescents, as well as, in general, the nature of ordering strategies in the acquisition of concepts (Hill 1974: 192).

We may be able to illuminate the picture of architectonic origins a bit more by contrasting the organizational properties of contemporary environments to the ordered environments of other species. The next section will briefly address some of the salient comparative evidence.

ZOOARCHITECTONICS

Other species construct habitats, often of a highly complex technological nature, as von Frisch and others have observed (von Frisch 1974; Wilson 1975:256). There appear, however, to be a number of significant differences between human and nonhuman habitats, although, clearly, we have a great deal yet to learn about both.

One of the more obvious apparent contrasts concerns flexibility and changeability, particularly with regard to media, but also with respect to functionality. Human built environments appear to be in a constant state of flux, replacement and growth. Formations and their interrelationships are subject to change, and rates of change cannot easily be matched by changes in function, purpose, and use, which often appear to have their own chronology and direction. Indeed, it often appears that the history of an architectonic system resembles an impossible game unfolding over time in which not only the tokens, but also the rules of play, are subject to change without notice. It is understandable that earlier generations of writers overcompensated for this apparent complexity by imposing rigidly defined ontogenetic categories simplistically modeled on biological and other analogs.[16]

The obvious question, of course, is whether or not the extreme variability in human habitats—both diachronically and diatopically—and taken as a potential point of contrast with nonhuman habitats, is more apparent than real. It would seem to be generically the case that, in the nonhuman world, change in habitat organization is accompanied by somatic variation, whereas in the human world such formative, architectonic variation contrasts with a uniform somatic radiation of the species.

For *homo sapiens*, in other words, geographic variation in built environments is not accompanied by significant changes in bodily morphology, and what differences there are among humans appear to reflect finely-calibrated distinctive responses to climatic conditions—skin pigmentation, hair structure, and so forth.

Moreover, variations among built environments cannot be unambiguously related to climatic factors, and appear to concern characteristic features of material organization or realization rather than formal typology (Preziosi 1979a; Chapter V). In terms of formal and conceptual organization, human habitats reveal a number of organizational features held in common, which have less to do with similarities in materialization than they have to do with underlying processes of formation, spatiality, and geometry.[17]

Thus a careful comparison of human and nonhuman habitats will have to address systems of *formative organization* in order to characterize those features common to our species, in a context of enormous material or medium variation and flexibility. Once again it is important to bear in mind that the medium of human built environments is potentially any set of environmental resources palpable to human vision and proprioception. In this regard, human and nonhuman habitats contrast sharply. Human architectonic systems appear to be inherently more sensitive to changes induced in a society from any quarter, and moreover exist as components in broader cultural systems organized as completely-integrated subsystems of communication and representation.

In another sense, human architectonic objects stand at one end of a continuum of increased multifunctionality and group-specific conventionality of association, thereby offering a marked contrast to the component constructs of other species, which to a greater or lesser degree are often invariantly determined in a one-to-one fashion with respect to behavioral association.

One area in which it is commonly supposed that human habitats differ strongly from nonhuman constructs is in the area of the transmission of information about processes of construction. While it often appears to be the case that the 'blueprints' of a non-human habitat are genetically fixed, requiring little or no learning, our increasing knowledge of zooarchitectonics suggests that the situation is highly complex, and varies from species to species (von Frisch 1974, *passim*; Alcock 1972:464 f.). It may be useful at this point to consider the role played by social learning in the construction of environments by our near relatives.

Of all animals presently extant, the chimpanzee seems most closely to resemble us in anatomy and mental capacity, although our relationships ontogenetically appear to be more parallel than linear; we may both possibly stem from a common early ancestor (Lancaster 1975:5). Despite certain similarities, the differences between us are quite striking in a number of respects.

But the chimpanzee also builds, and moreover learns the skills of building by observation and example. As early as ten months of age, chimps have been observed (by J. van Lawick-Goodall and others) (van Lawick-Goodall 1971; Kohler 1926; von Frisch 1974:278 ff.) to begin making sleeping nests by observing and imitating adults. By the age of four or five years, the youngster has become proficient at building his own nest and has begun to sleep away from his mother's nest.

The sleeping nest consists of a firm foundation in the fork of a tree-crotch within which small twigs and branches are bent to form a soft cushion, to be pressed into place by the weight of the body. Normally, a new nest is built each evening, although this depends upon the foraging habits of the troop: occasionally an individual will use the same tree and tree-crotch for several nights at a stretch.

Chimpanzees also manifest other constructional skills, as observed by a number of writers, including Kohler. They will often build temporary platforms out of available material in order to reach some food source otherwise out of arm's length. In such a case, the individual is reordering elements of his environment to achieve some specific aim (normally related to food gathering (Alcock 1972:465 ff.). This behavioral characteristic is closely related to toolmaking and tool use (in the manner suggested above): the construction serves *pro tempore* as a means to achieve a specific goal, in a manner equivalent to using a stick or probe to pry open a food source such as termites, ants, or the honey of a nest of bees.

Chimpanzees build temporary (individual) dwellings (sleeping nests), and they assemble and construct objects to facilitate some desirable end (collecting otherwise unreachable food) (Lancaster 1975:42-55). Both of these activities are realizations of the generic tendencies of primates to manipulate objects in an environment. Furthermore, much of this activity appears to be socially learned. Indeed, it would appear that primates learn to communicate in general through social imitation.

But chimpanzees apparently do not use sleeping nests for other activities, and the morphological format of a sleeping nest—its design—remains invariant from one generation to another, and such changes as occur from one nest to another (when made by the same individual) are accidental properties induced by the details of a given tree.

In contrast, a given architectonic formation made by humans characteristically frames activities of various kinds, in a greater or lesser degree according to the conventional rules of association of a given group or society. Even when a certain spatial formation is characteristically associated with a given behavior complex in a group over time, that association is inherently conventional rather than invariant, and is subject to alteration at any time. Such a formation exists in an ordered set of contrastive formations, and its functional identity is determined by a network of associations. Moreover, an apparently identical formation may have very different associations for another group downstream (by definition, then, it is not the *same* formation).

The human architectonic formation, in other words, manifests a dual significance, defined, on the one hand, by characteristic associations between a formation and its conventionally determined, extraarchitectonic behavioral reference, and, on the other hand, by its systemic function as a sign in an ordered system of signs.

It is becoming increasingly evident that it would be patently simplistic to picture the emergence of the human built environment as an elaboration of only one kind of activity in the primate background—for example nest building as manifest in chimpanzee behavior, or of territorial behavior among primates in general. It can only have arisen within the content of a generalized communicative-semiotic activity, and in concert with a variety of other code systems (most especially verbal language) in the manner suggested in previous sections. In ways we do not yet clearly understand, the generalized behavior-matrix which served as the background to the emergence of the built environment must have comprised sets of behavioral traits which had come to be seen as conceptually equivalent and partly redundant. The tendency to see an environment *mark* as a *sign* and as a *tool*, and to see a tool as a sign, as well as a concurrent or concomitant tendency to see a vocal sign as a tool or as a mark,[18] must have paved the way for the coalescence of multimodal behaviors out of which emerged an ordered set of semiotic codes designed to interact with each other so as to provide overlapping perspectives on a common sociocultural reality.

In the next chapter, we shall look at the question of the emergence of the built environment from the perspective of the multiple *roles* played by architectonic objects.

NOTES

1. See below, Chapter IV, and R. Jakobson and L. R. Waugh (1979); R. Jakobson and M. Halle (1956).
2. Discussed in detail below in Chapter IV, and in D. Preziosi (1979a, Chapters II, III, and Appendix B).
3. On the subject of sense-discriminative and sense-determinative signs in verbal language, see Jakobson and Waugh (1979).
4. On Olduvai, see W. A. Fairservis (1975:58).

5. See above, Chapter I, Note 4.
6. On gestural signing, the best source of bibliography will be found in M. R. Key (1975, 1977); A. Siegman and S. Feldstein (1978); R. Wescott, ed. (1974), especially chapters by W. Stokoe, pp. 35-68.
7. D. Preziosi (1979a, Appendix A; 1978); M. Silverstein (1976:11-56).
8. Discussed below in Chapter III.
9. See S. B. Petrovich and E. H. Hess (1978) for a summary of various possible scenarios, and C. F. Hockett and R. Ascher (1964).
10. On linguistic embedding, see U. Weinreich (1966:142 ff., esp. 190 f.).
11. Discussed by U. Neisser (1976:166 ff.).
12. Neisser (1976:154 ff.); see also T. G. R. Bower (1977), especially Chapters 5 and 7.
13. See T. Hawkes (1977:134); J. Mukarovsky (1978:236 ff.).
14. On this subject in general see Yi-Fu Tuan (1975, *passim*).
15. D. Preziosi (1979a, Appendix B; and below, Chapter IV).
16. A useful discussion of the history of 'architectural history' in terms of changing metaphorical models may be found in P. Collins (1965).
17. See A. Rapoport (1969) for a discussion of climatic and geographical deterministic models.
18. This subject will be taken up in more detail below in Chapter VI.

3

The Functions of the Built Environment

MULTIFUNCTIONALITY

Communicative acts in any signaling medium are inherently complex, involving interactions among a variety of constituent factors. A message in any one medium seldom, if ever, contains all of the 'meaning' of a transaction, for meaningfulness is a function of the totality of relationships manifested in a communicative event. Such events, in normaly daily-life semiosis, incorporate a variety of media and modalities, each of which contributes in its own fashion to the totality.

Meaning does not exist in an aprioristic manner, as an entity 'carried' by a given signalization, any more than formations exist apart from their significations. In addition, meaningfulness is invariably oriented toward one or more of the component parts of a transmission—toward the referential context, toward either the generator or the receiver, toward the signalization itself, or simply toward the maintenance of contact between encoder and decoder. In addition, any message constitutes an interrogation of or commentary upon the code of which it is a manifestation.

Meaningfulness, in other words, is invariably indexical with respect to one or more of the component parts of a transmissive act.

It is evidently the case that any semiotic system incorporates formations whose significance cannot be entirely disambiguated without indexical reference to the signing context. In verbal language, there exist in every system encoded elements whose meanings 'shift' from one referent to another depending upon the actual interpersonal context of the speech-act—for example personal pronouns.[1] But while it is the case that every language contains 'shifters' encoded as such, the phenomenon of deixis potentially implicates almost any aspect of the code.

With respect to the multifunctional aspect of the architectonic code, perhaps the most lucid and insightful explication of the nature of meaningfulness in the built environment has been that of Jan Mukařovský who, writing in 1938, delimited what he termed the five functional horizons of architecture (Mukařovský 1978: 236 ff.).

Architecture, he states, organizes space with respect to man in his entirety, with respect to all the physical and psychic activities of which he is capable. In organizing space as a whole, none of the parts of architecture has functional independence; all of its functions are interdependent and mutually implicative.

A building's function is determined by (1) an immediate purpose —its usage-context; (2) an historical purpose, wherein functionality is 'governed not only by an immediate practical consideration but also by a fixed canon (or set of norms) for this kind of structure and its previous development (Mukařovský 1978:242). In other words, any architectonic formation is in a variety of ways a referential commentary upon its own preexistent code.

In addition, a building manifests a functional horizon which is (3) created by 'the organization of the collective to which the client and architect belong, in accordance with the organization of society, the available economic and material possibilities, and so forth',[2] That is to say, a building also exists as a manifestation of the identity and territoriality of its users and makers, and contributes to the maintenance of that association.

Mukarovsky also refers to the aesthetic function of architectonic artifacts, wherein, when this function is in dominance, (4) it 'renders the thing itself as the purpose' (Mukařovský 1978:244). In his discussion of the aesthetic function both in the aforementioned essay and elsewhere (Mukařovský 1936 [1970]), he notes that there is not an object-type which necessarily has to be the vehicle of this function: any formation or activity is potentially aesthetic in function. In the aesthetic function, a dominance of focus is upon the signalization itself.

The fifth architectonic function is what is termed the individual functional horizon, wherein 'an individual can obviously deviate from everything which has been set as a norm by the preceding horizons (Mukařovský 1978:242). He sees this as a violation of functionality deriving from the decision of an individual, whether client or architect.

There exist, however, a number of significant differences between the two types of 'violations', as we shall see, and it is in this area that the writer's picture of architectonic function becomes somewhat ambiguous. The situation may be clarified by considering the nature of architectonic signing itself: is the designer (or builder) an 'encoder' as against a user who might be a 'decoder'? Who is addressing whom? Before discussing this problem, let us look at the question of multifunctionality from a broader semiotic perspective.

It will be clear that Mukařovský's 'functional horizons' not only implicate various copresent components in the act of transmission of any architectonic formation, they also bear a close correlation with the several component elements in any linguistic transmission. As formulated by Jakobson, there exist six constituent elements in any speech act:[3]

the addresser
the addressee
the message
the code
the referential context
the contact between speaker and hearer

Corresponding to the six elements of a speech-act, he distinguishes six corresponding functions:

1. orientation toward the addresser: *emotive* function
   ('Ithaca is terribly far from New York');
2. orientation toward the addressee: *conative* function
   ('Why don't you drive up to Ithaca tomorrow'?);
3. orientation toward the message: *poetic* function
   ('Good night/sleep tight/don't let the bed bugs bite');
4. orientation toward the code: *metalinguistic* function
   ('Did you say New York or Newark'?);

5. orientation toward the context: *referential* function
   ('Ithaca is 250 miles from New York'); and
6. orientation toward contact: *phatic* function
   ('Hello Mr. and Mrs. America and all the ships at sea').

Normally, in an utterance, a *variety* of functions are copresent, each with varying degrees of *dominance*, correlating with a dominance of *focus* upon one or more of the copresent components of the speech event.

In a speech-act, a speaker himself will produce a formation through the instrumentality of his own speech organs. In the built environment, there may be a personal distinction between what are traditionally referred to as a 'designer' and 'builder(s)'. In other words, the initiator of an architectonic transmission may not in fact 'construct' that transmission, but may instead present to others for realization a simulative model or diagram or set of instructions (verbal or graphic) of the intended transmission. Those 'others' may include the 'client' himself.

On the other side, the intended receiver of the transmission may be the transmitter himself (as may also be the case with a verbal utterance) or one or more others. Once formed, an architectonic formation continues to broadcast widely (unlike a speech-act, which decays instantaneously unless otherwise recorded). Moreover, the personal identity of the receivers is not necessarily constant, and generations of individuals may continue to 'receive' an archaic transmission. There exists an 'object permanence' in architectonic signing—a permanence which is relative to linguistic signing. Furthermore, because an architectonic formation may become intersubjectively appropriated by groups of individuals, the various referential associations of a given formation may change over time, whether or not the construct is materially altered.

A necessary corollary of this situation is the fact that architectonic evolution is in no way linear in itself, but is (as is the case with any semiotic system in its diachrony) a function of the complexly integrated and cumulative evolution of a culture itself, in its totality.[4]

In an architectonic code, the initial generator of a formation may be a person or persons who design a formation who may also (but not necessarily) construct that formation for a client (who may be the generator or builder) who employs that formation significantly (and thus serves as a transmitter of that signal to himself or others). While in an idealized sense, and in a manner analogous to the 'speaker-hearer' transmission in verbal language, there exists an 'addresser' and an 'addressee', as well as a (more or less permanent) 'message' or transmission, the nature of the architectonic medium, as well as its mode of perceptual address, suggest that the correlative 'addresser' in architectonic semiosis is the *user*(s) of a given formation.

The situation is thereby rather more complex than the idealized encoder-decoder relationship in speech-acts, despite a generic functional correlativity between the two semiotic codes. Thus, in the built environment, the processes of behavioral appropriation align with those of 'reading' on the linguistic side: but this is not to affirm that the built environment stands parallel, semiotically, to the processes of 'reading' a text (where texts are construed to mean simple recordings of linguistic utterances), for a built environment constitutes a primary sign-system in its own right. These differences are induced principally by the nature of the signing medium itself and its (relative) object permanence. In other respects, moreover, a patent correlativity exists between the two codes with regard to multifunctional focus upon the various component parts of a transmission.

Consequently, Mukařovský's 'functional deviation' on the part of 'addressees' cannot, strictly speaking, be considered a 'function' in and of the code itself except insofar as there exist (as in any code) a certain contextual variation in appropriative usage.

An architectonic formation may reveal an emphasis upon various aspects of the identity and internal states of signers themselves —as in the case where a formation manifests sense-determinative cues regarding the orientation of the signers upon the various components of architectonic semiosis. A formation may bear the mark of a personal 'style' through palpable variations in the realization of corpus-specific norms, or of common referential associations, or aesthetic norms.

Such an orientation patently recalls the 'emotive' functions of a given linguistic utterance, wherein a speaker will give cues as to his particular orientation upon a given subject. The emotive orientation of a speech-act may be perceptually cued by a wide variety of code-specific means—intonation, stress, the incorporation of particular lexical units, etc.

In a similar fashion, an architectonic formation patently reveals an emotive or expressive orientation upon the identity and state of an 'addresser' (maker and/or user) through code-specific means. An outsider or a child may have to learn a large number of subtle cues as to whether a given formation manifests a personal, expressive, stylistic orientation *vis-a-vis* a conventional set of norms. Such cues may implicate details of geometric or spatial features, the use of characteristic materials, colors, textures, and norms of usage and appropriation. If kitchens are conventionally 1:1:1 cubic cells, and bedrooms 1:3:1 cells, then a formation in that code which reverses these proportions and contextual associations may be expressive of the particular perspective on these norms by makers. Similarly, a reversed appropriation of these made cells on the part of a user or users induces a similar expressive orientation.

Also, the architectonic correlate of the linguistic 'addresser' may be either the user or users themselves (*vis-à-vis* other builders), or those apart from the user with respect to whom the user appropriates a formation in significative fashion (which may also include solely the user himself). That architectonic formations are employed in a conative, exhortatory or directive manner is patent. Certain behaviors are staged or induced through the spatiotemporal organization of given constructs, and environmental objects carry exhortations to channel, constrain and routinize spatiokentic activity. However 'loosely' organized, no architectonic formation permits every possible behavior or conceptual association. In an architectonic code there will exist a wide variety of means which implicate a focus upon the 'addressees', which prescribe certain readings, and which induce proper or canonical orientations upon interpretation. In many codes, it is often the case that a building (despite its highly complex tridimensional organization) prescribes a proper reading, whether through geometric or spatial organization, modularities of material, etc. From a given standpoint or perspective, the entire composition may fall into line or make compositional sense. Thus in the Roman Pantheon, the recessed ceiling coffers in the great dome are so modeled as to appear symmetrical and perpendicular to their outer surfaces from one central point only—namely the center of the floor, the prescribed place for worship of the pantheon of divinities whose shrines are arrayed around the circular drum walls. It is only from this point that the great domed ceiling appears harmoniously composed.

Any architectonic formation incorporates sets of 'instructions' for proper reading, and directly addresses its users. The means for doing this are widely various, and may also be achieved cross-modally, by means of written signs and graphic devices ('exit', 'don't go down the up staircase', etc.).

By virtue of the fact that an architectonic formation necessarily channels behavior in a variety of ways, the phatic or 'territorial' function of an environmental artifact is often coexistent with its conative or directive function. Buildings induce information regarding the collectivity of a social group, its group identity, and they prescribe, augment, and perceptually enhance that collectivity. But the phatic/territorial and conative functions are not coterminous, and, in part, the distinction between them lies in the vector of emphasis.

Linguistic conation comprises exhortation which is only in part territorial or addressed *to* spatiokinesis; architectonic conation addresses 'addressees' *through* spatiokinetic organization to achieve a variety of conceptual ends.

Architectonic objects function territorially by staging behavioral episodes or routines, framing interpersonal interaction, and dividing, structuring, delimiting, or zoning an environment. Once again, the means whereby this is achieved are corpus-specific, involving a great many different kinds of formative activity—use of color, textures, gradations of size and consistencies of shape, etc. Some architectonic objects may reveal a predominance of phaticism or territoriality (a neighborhood well or chapel, walls, grown hedges, shopping streets, and so forth). But here again, as with all other architectonic functions, the territorial function of an object necessarily coexists with other functions (wells and chapels have referential contexts or usages, etc.).

A building additionally may reveal a predominance of orientation upon its own signalization or composition, thereby implicating the aesthetic function, correlative to the poetic usage of any speech-act. As with other functions, what constitutes a dominance of aesthetic orientation is *code-specific* with respect to the norms of that code at a specific time and place. In order to understand what is aesthetic about a given formation, one must know the code of which that formation is a realization.

The site of aesthetic functionality necessarily shifts over time and geography, even within the same code: at one period it may be predominant in religious or governmental constructs, at another in private dwellings or the modularities of street architecture.[5] It may involve harmonies of color, texture, medium, geometric shape, or compositional arrangement of environmental components.

Moreover, it is not necessarily the case that the aesthetic function is inherently associated with one or another building *type*: no one formational type in a code is inherently more prone to manifest a dominance of the aesthetic function than any other, even if it may be the case that for a given corpus at a particular time and place there may be characteristic associations. The aesthetic function is the potential property of any building type, and there may be no abrupt boundary between structures with an aesthetic function predominant and those with which it plays a lesser role.

Another function manifest by architectonic formations involves an orientation upon the code itself of which they are a manifestation. Normally this is realized architectonically through historical reference or allusion. Indeed, any architectonic object comprises a commentary upon and interrogation of its own code. The allusory or meta-codal function, patently correlative to the metalinguistic function of verbal utterances, may take many different forms, from pedantic recreations of famous landmarks, such as a copy of a classical temple (which may, however, manifest for its referential context nonhistorical usages, such as a bank or stock exchange, etc.) to formations whose outer facade alone simulates an historical prototype, or presents a transformation of its received symbolisms. The allusions, moreover, may be cross-codal, as in the case of a restaurant in an European city whose component parts purport to represent a Polynesian hut.

A formation may function meta-codally to a very minimal degree, wherein allusory reference is confined to details of material articulation such as baseboard mouldings or the paneling of doorways, or where the triglyph-metope frieze of a classical stone temple simulates wooden prototypes, or where the spatial or facade proportions of a villa by Le Corbusier may allude to those of Renaissance villas while being abruptly different in other respects.

In addition, architectonic formations incorporate a contextually-referential function, a 'usage' in the traditional sense, wherein a variety of behavioral activities are differentially cued by building types or by spatiotemporal compositions. The immediate 'purpose(s)' or contextual 'utility' of a formation, as with its linguistic referential correlate, is necessarily embedded in the other five functions just noted.

The meaningfulness of an architectonic formation, then, is inherently multidimensional; every function necessarily coexists with others, in varying degrees of dominance. No architectonic object is 'purely' one or another. The differential dominance of varying functions necessarily induces a different 'mix' of functionality, and there is no inherent hierarchy among architectonic functions.

As a semiotic code, the architectonic system is inherently *relational* in aspect and organization.

A semiotic perspective on the built environment, then, induces a picture of meaningfulness abruptly different from that portrayed in traditional stylistic analysis or iconography, while at the same time incorporating received notions of architectonic meaning in a more powerful, systematic, and realistic manner. It implicates the notion of 'style' as a loose aggregate of various aspects of functionality, overlapping several architectonic 'horizons' or functional categories. Through its insistence upon a holistic consideration of the question of meaning, it renders obsolete the received art-historical notions of meaning, and provides an integrated picture of the built environment in its totality, through its rejection of the form/content dualism inherent both in traditional architectural analysis and atomistic ('shopping bag') structuralism.

FUNCTIONAL CORRELATIVITY

These observations may be summarized by the following outline of the *correlativity* of functionality in architectonic and linguistic semiosis.

| *Architectonic semiosis* | | | *Linguistic semiosis* | | |
orientation	function		orientation		function
context	:	referential	: :	context	:	referential
formation	:	aesthetic	: :	message	:	poetic
code	:	allusory	: :	code	:	metalinguistic
contact	:	territorial	: :	contact	:	phatic
'addresser'	:	expressive	: :	speaker	:	emotive
'addressee'	:	directive	: :	hearer	:	conative

It will be clear, in our discussion in the previous section, that such correlations comprise broad *systemic* equivalencies, given the patent differences between the two codes in the nature of the signing media, their relative object-permanences, mode of perceptual address, as well as the complexities inherent in the 'addresser-addressee' relationship in architectonic semiosis. The two codes are not isofunctional in any given culture, and their redundancies overlap in a dynamic fashion. They are not two ways of 'doing the same things', and they are partly redundant and semiautonomous modalities in daily-life multimodal semiotic behavior. Each is designed to interact with the other in a variety of ways, while simultaneously offering different advantages under contrastive sociocultural circumstances. Whatever architectonic and linguistic systems share, they share features by virtue of their generic functions as panhuman sign-systems. Each provides a partially-overlapped perspective on the totalities of a society's culture.

We cannot adequately understand the structure and operant functions of either modality without an understanding of its cross-indexed complement and supplement. The picture of architectonic multifunctionality elaborated here will necessarily alter and broaden our understanding of the multifunctional nature of the speech signal, and deepen our understanding of the semiotic foundations of culture itself.

But such a deepening of our understanding will be short-circuited if we regard either sign-system as merely a parallel, transitively commutative translation of the one into the other. Each is the realization of the globality of our semiotic intelligence as manifested differentially in various modalities. And each is deeply embedded in the other: buildings implicate texts and utterances as much as speech acts implicate environmental contexts and their spatiokinetic affordances. Each is unthinkable without the other. In the next chapter we shall outline briefly the nature of the formative organization of the architectonic code as presently understood.

NOTES

1. See R. Jakobson (1971b:130-147); see also M. Silverstein (1976:11 ff.).
2. In Mukařovský (1978:242) the writer further suggests that various nuances of the symbolic function are incorporated here.
3. See R. Jakobson (1960:350-377).
4. See below, Chapter V, and Chapter IV, Note 9.
5. As discussed by Mukařovský (1936 [1970]:1-22).

4

The Form of the Built Environment

Everything about an architectonic formation is meaningful in some way, but not everything is meaningful in the same way.

Architectonic objects comprise patterned, tridimensionally-syntagmatic arrays articulated by means of code-specific and rule-governed contrasts and oppositions among masses, spaces, materials, colors, textures, and relative sizes. Distinctions and disjunctions in formation exist to cue the perception of differences in meaning. The elements in an architectonic array are defined by perceptually-palpable edges, boundaries, and other contrasts and discontinuities. Moreover, a built environment is spatiotemporal in organization: only a portion of an architectonic formation is perceptually palpable from any one stance or perspective. A building or street unfolds over time, and its significance is cued temporally as well as spatially. In contrast to audition, which is omnidirectional, vision is directional; an object of even minimal complexity is used ('read') over time.

Built environments are composed to address the directionality and temporality of vision. They are read piecemeal, over time. An architectonic object is not a static stage set or backdrop, and every component of a formation indexically and metonymically implicates the reading of adjacent components, both visible and potentially visible. In addition to this syntagmatic association among architectonic components, formations are related paradigmatically to others which are not immediately copresent but which may potentially occupy equivalent positions in an array.

In connection with an ongoing research program concerned with the semiotic analysis of built environments, a provisional picture of the formative systematicity of the architectonic code has begun to emerge,[1] and for the first time we may be in a reasonably secure position to discuss the nature of minimal significative units in architectonic codes, as well as the hierarchical network of sign-types and their operant interactions.

The present chapter will present a summary of these findings, and will offer a tentative comparison of architectonic and linguistic sign-types, on the basis of evidence to date.

THE NETWORK OF ARCHITECTONIC SIGNS

Architectonic analysis necessarily has as its focus the sum of co-present formations comprising a given environment in a synchronic sense, rather than 'typical', 'exemplary', or (extrinsically) noteworthy 'monuments'. A semiotic analysis of a built environment eschews the piecemeal examination of portions of environments typical of 'architectural history' with its stress upon impressionistically noteworthy 'milestones' in diachronic development.

Forms do not have a life of their own apart from their significative contexts, and buildings only form linked series through time in a cumulative rather than unilinear or genaeological sense. The 'history' of architecture is a selective fiction, and the linkage of architecture to the 'history' of 'art' is a doubly-confounded academic misconstrual both of the nature of aesthetic activity and of the built environment. A semiotic perspective on the analysis of built environments redresses the formalistic organicism of architectural diachrony by its focus upon the synchronic systematicity of the built environment of a culture.

Recent analyses have made a strong case for the existence of two types of signs in the architectonic code, on the basis of a fundamental differentiation of their *signata*. Components of a built environment are either directly or indirectly significative, a distinction based upon the nature of the relationship between *signantia* and *signata*.

This distinction parallels the systemic distinction in verbal language between *signantia* which signal that two words are different in meaning without signaling what the meaning difference is, and those which convey specific units of information. In the case of the former, a given *signans* (e.g. a distinctive feature or a phoneme) carries a systemic significance with respect to its role in the building of directly significative elements (e.g. morphemes, words, phrases, sentences, discourses).

This design property of 'duality of patterning' or double articulation is common to both the architectonic and linguistic codes:[2] in each system there exist encoded units of two types—those with indirect signification and those with direct signification.

In both codes, signals are arrayed in syntagmatically-sequential fashion along templates comprising patterns of alternatively-juxtaposed entities which contrast with each other on the basis of contrastive, distinctive features. In built environments, such *templates* comprise patterns of aggregation of *signantia* according to perceptually-palpable, binarily-encoded contrasts between two features or attributes of visible formations—opacity and transparency.[3] In an architectonic artifact, component parts are either opaque or transparent. This contrast among distinctive features is less an all-or-none contrast and more of a 'greater-vs.-lesser' contrast, and it is realized differentially in different systems, depending upon the network of features present in a given code, and their rule-governed interrelations. This is not exactly tantamount to suggesting that two types of forms exist in architectonic codes—e.g. mass forms and space forms—for it is patent that some 'mass' forms may be transparent, such as glass, or translucent, such as cloth.[4] In other words, opacity and transparency are not coterminous, as attributes of form, with 'mass' an 'space'.

As a *signans*, the *template* consists of the syntagmatic juxtaposition of forms which—however else they may differ—contrast by at least this one feature.

The *signatum* of a *template* is sensory discrimination *per se*. It has no singleness of reference in itself apart from its indirect signification *vis-a-vis* the building of *signantia* with direct signification.

Alternative patterning in the architectonic code is systemically correlative to linguistic syllabification—i.e. the alternative juxtaposition of phonemes or phoneme-clusters which contrast by at least one distinctive feature—namely consonantalism or vocalism.

Just as the opacity/transparency contrastive opposition applies to every architectonic conformation, so is it the case that every phonemic entity in the linguistic code manifests a distinctive feature of either vocalism or consonantalism.[5]

In both codes, alternative patterning is sense-discriminative, existing specifically to address sensory perception, whether visual or auditory. In the linguistic code, alternative patterning is syntagmatically-sequential and unilinear, in accordance with the temporality of auditory perception, while in the architectonic code it is tridimensionally syntagmatic and sequential, and spatiotemporal.

Both the *template* and the syllable are built out of encoded units which are themselves sense-discriminative and indirectly significative. In the linguistic code, the syllable is composed of sequential arrays of phonemes, which are themselves comprised of bundles or clusters of syntagmatically-simultaneous distinctive features. Phonemes are distinguished from each other on the basis of differences among particular mixes of copresent distinctive features. A distinctive feature is an attribute of sound which signals that a given word in which it occurs is different from any other word in the given language endowed with a different property.

There exists a hierarchy of sign-types of a sense-discriminative nature in the linguistic code, from minimal encoded *signantia* such as distinctive features, to phonemes, encoded as syntagmatically-simultaneous clusters of features, to syllables, encoded as syntagmatically-sequential alternations of phonemes manifesting juxtaposed distinctive features of consonantalism and vocalism.

In the architectonic code, evidence has now accumulated for the existence of a systemically correlative hierarchy of sign-types of a sense-discriminative nature. *Templates* are built out of syntagmatically-sequential arrays of *forms* which are themselves contrasted with each other on the basis of contrasts among syntagmatically-simultaneous clusters of distinctive *features*, the latter including not only opacity and transparency (which between them bifurcate the whole system of features), but an entire range of sensory attributes of conformation such as geometric configuration, color-oppositions (themselves encoded perceptually as sets of binary contrasts),[6] relative gradiencies of texture and planar articulation, as well as modularities of size. All of these features are defined according to the conventions of a particular architectonic system.

One of the most important revelations in recent architectonic analysis has been the indication that the number of *forms* in a corpus at a given place and time is not only finite, but fairly small. An illustration of this is given in Figure 1, which portrays the set of *forms* in one code (Minoan, ± 1500 BC), considered from the perspective of contrastive oppositions among several distinctive features.

Such *forms* are not directly significative in themselves, but serve to distinguish entities in the code with direct (sense-determinative) signification. Sense-determinative units comprise a network of signs in the architectonic system which comprise a second hierarchy. The maximal sense-determinative or directly-significative sign-type encoded as such is what has come to be termed the *cell*, consisting of syntagmatic arrays of *templates* of *forms* spatiotemporally aggregated. The notion of the *cell* is not coterminous with that of a 'space-cell' or room (mass-bounded space), but rather comprises a topological unicum composed of one or more templates tridimensionally arrayed, as suggested in Figure 2. below.

The *cell* is the 'largest' directly-significative unit encoded as such in a given code. Strictly speaking, however, it is not made up of *templates*, but rather of aggregates of minimal sense-determinative units termed *figures*, which themselves may comprise any of the three types of sense-discriminative signs or clusters thereof. It has become patent in architectonic analysis that the hierarchized differences in meaning in a code are not necessarily correlated with consistently hierarchized differences in formation. In other words, in an architectonic code it is *not* the case that the hierarchy of sign types involves merely sets of increasingly 'larger' entities. In the network of sense-determinative units, there is no direct correlation between differentiation in the *signans* and differentiation in the *signatum*.

A *figure* may be anything from a *feature* to a *form* to a *template* to a code-specific and rule-governed array of several of these. Its *signantia* may be quite various.

In a given built environment, direct signification may be signaled by a wide variety of conformations, from specific geometric forms (spatial or massive) to gradiencies or contrasts in the size of geometric forms, to the presence of given media, colors, textures, or patterned arrangements of any of these. The nature and identity

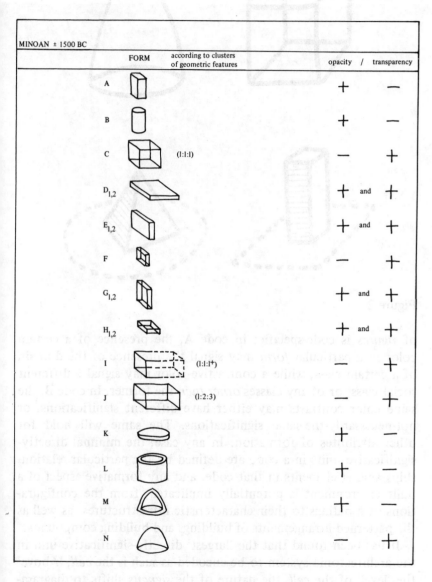

MINOAN ± 1500 BC	FORM	according to clusters of geometric features	opacity	/	transparency
A			+		−
B			+		−
C		(1:1:1)	−		+
D$_{1,2}$			+	and	+
E$_{1,2}$			+	and	+
F			−		+
G$_{1,2}$			+	and	+
H$_{1,2}$			+	and	+
I		(1:1:1$^+$)	−		+
J		(1:2:3)	−		+
K			+		−
L			+		−
M			+		−
N					+

Figure 1.

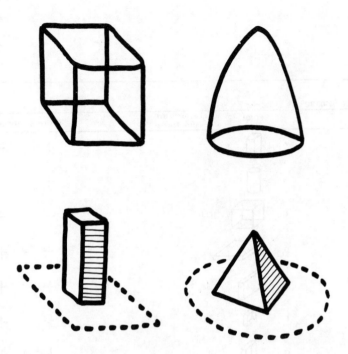

Figure 2.

of *figures* is code-specific: in code A, the presence of a certain color in a particular *form* may signal the presence of the domain of a certain class, while a contrastive color may signal a different social class, or of any classes *other than* the former. In code B, the same color contrasts may either have different significations, or not-necessarily-the-same significations. The same will hold for other attributes of formation. In any case, the minimal directly-significative units in a code are defined by the particular relationships among elements in that code, and any formative aspect of a built environment is potentially implicated, from the configurations of buildings to their characteristic infrastructures, as well as the patterned arrangements of buildings and building compounds.

It has been found that the 'largest' directly-significative unit in the architectonic system to be encoded as such is the *cell*. 'Above' the 'level' of the *cell*, the nature of the *signans* shifts to diagrammatic patterns of aggregation of *cells*, what have come to be termed *matrices*.

A *matrix* comprises a syntagmatically-sequential aggregation of *cells*—encoded specifications as to canonical juxtapositions (tridimensionally and spatiotemporally) of cellular units, with respect to their topological connectivities. Examples of *matrices* in two different codes are given below in Figure 3. In *A*, a typical *matrix* forming a portion of a standard dwelling unit in the code portrayed in Figure 1 above is given. The *matrix* includes not only the specification of certain types of *cells*—i.e. having particular contrastive geometric configurations—but also the nature of their relationship to other *cells* or *matrices*. Thus, a canonical 90° change in direction from the direction of entrance into a house is an invariant property of this particular *matrix* type.[7]

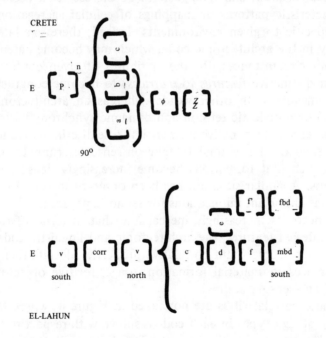

E : exterior   p : primary access   φ: one cell   Ƶ̲: stairwell
v̲: vestibule   corr̲: corridor   fbd̲ : women's quarter   mbd̲ : men's quarter
a,b,c̲ : hall system   c,d,e,f,f' : hypostyle hall system

Figure 3.

In *B*, a contemporary code in Middle Kingdom Egypt reveals a different *matrix* form in an equivalent (domestic) setting. Here, one of the invariant properties of the *matrix* is its alignment along a north-to-south axis, in addition to the code-specific specifications regarding the geometric form of the *cells* arrayed as well as their relative sizes (progressing from larger *cells* to smaller on the north-south axis of the building.[8]

As patterns of aggregation of sense-determinative signs, *matrices* themselves enter into patterned aggregates. It is patent that an architectonic code is increasingly creative and productive 'above' the level of the *matrix*. There also exists a tendency for *matrices* to become characteristically 'fixed' over time in an idiomatic or habitual fashion, and it appears to be the case that users encode characteristic patterns or mappings of cellular aggregation which are specific to given environments. Indeed, there is a latent tendency in the architectonic code, which may become patent under certain circumstances, for the attributes of given conformations (from distinctive *features* to *matrices*) to become congruent with their meanings. In other words, whereas an architectonic code manifests a dialectic tension and dynamic synchrony with respect to its sense-determinative *vis-a-vis* its sense-discriminative features, over time the latter tend to take on sense-determinative associations such that formations become increasingly dense and polysemous. A similar situation has been observed in verbal language, and has important implications for semiotic phylogeny.[9]

It becomes increasingly inescapable that in terms of their systemic design features, the architectonic and linguistic codes share a number of important correlative properties, despite their abrupt differences in material formation, usage, relative object-permanence, and sensory address.

These correlativities are portrayed in Figure 4, where the hierarchy of sign types in each code is shown with respect to the relational position of their *signantia*. The diagram illustrates that the relationship between an architectonic *figure* and a linguistic *morpheme* is not direct, but systemic: a *figure* bears a relationship to a *cell* that a *morpheme* bears to a *word*.

Signs of type *A* are minimal sense-discriminative units, encoded as paradigmatic binary oppositions among attributes or features of formation. Their *signata* are differentiatedness *per se*.

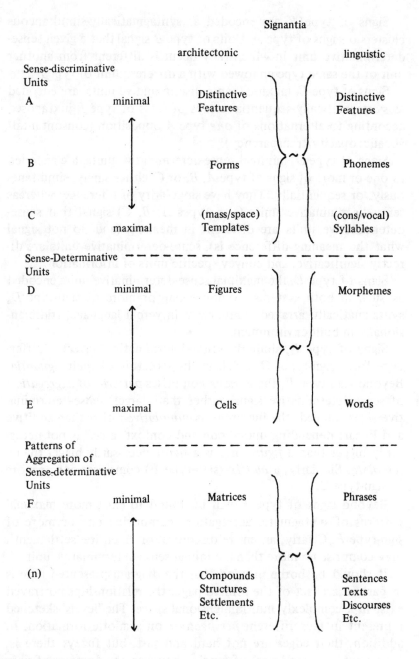

Figure 4.

Signs of type B are encoded as syntagmatically-simultaneous clusters of signs of type A. Units of type B signal that a given sense-determinative unit in which they occur is different from another unit of the same type endowed with a different unit of type B.

Signs of type C, maximal sense-discriminative units, are encoded as syntagmatically-sequential arrays of signs of type B juxtaposed according to alternations of *one* type A opposition (consontantal/vocalic; opacity/transparency).

Signs of type D, minimal sense-determinative units, are encoded as one or more of signs of type A, B, or C, either singly, simultaneously, or sequentially. They have singularity of reference: whereas sense-discriminative units (sign types A, B, C) signal that sense-determinative units are different in meaning (and do not signal what the meaning difference is), sense-determinative units are directly significative, and convey specific units of information.[10]

Signs of type E, the maximal sense-determinative units encoded as such in both systems, comprise one or more of sign-type D, syntagmatically arrayed: unilinearly in verbal language, tridimensionally in built environments.

Signs of type F, similarly sense-determinative, reveal a difference from sign-types D and E in the structure of their *signantia*. Beyond sign-type E, the *signans* comprises *patterns of aggregation* of sense-determinative signs, rather than 'larger' sense-determinative signs. Indeed, the hierarchy is *cumulative* rather than additive and linear: depending upon code and context, a *cell* is not necessarily bigger than a *figure*, nor is a *figure* necessarily bigger than a *template*. Similarly, a *matrix* (sign-type F) comprises one or more of sign-type E.

Beyond signs of type F will be found to exist more maximal patterns of syntagmatic aggregation, comprising one or more of sign-type F. Clearly, an entire discourse, or an entire 'settlement', may comprise no more than a minimal sense-determinative unit.

It should be borne in mind that the diagram presented here is in part an artifact of the printed page: the relationships portrayed exist in a complexly multidimensional space. The 'levels' sketched represent in fact different *perspectives* on semiotic formation. In addition, their edges are not hard and fast, but fuzzy: there is, for example, a good deal of overlap between the domains of sign-types E and F.

Clearly, an architectonic *cell* in no way resembles a linguistic lexical unit such as a word. But a *cell* bears a *systemic* relationship to other sign-types in its code that a word bears in its code: it is precisely in this sense that the two codes may be productively compared and contrasted, and their correlativities of design may be systematically revealed.

At the beginning of this chapter it was observed that everything about an architectonic formation is meaningful in some way, but that not everything is meaningful in the same way. In the light of the discussion above, it will be apparent that what was meant was that, whereas all architectonic signs, from features to settlements, have a *signatum*, they differ as to the *type* of *signatum*. In addition, the nature of the *signans* differs, depending upon the sign-type—from formative units encoded as such to patterns of aggregation among encoded units.

Moreover, it is patent that the hierarchized differences in *signata* are not necessarily correlated with consistently hierarchized differences in *signantia*. This pervasive asymmetry of patterning is a manifestation of the inherently *relational* nature of the architectonic code in *every* aspect of its organization. Indeed, it is only from a relational semiotic perspective that any aspect of the built environment can begin to make any sense at all. The signs in a code are a function of the systemic properties of a code *as a whole*: a code is not 'built up of' signs any more than a house is built of bricks.

NOTES

1. A project on the semiotic analysis of built environments was begun by the writer at Yale University in 1970, continued since 1973 at MIT and Cornell. A detailed report of progress to date will be found in D. Preziosi (1979a). The present summary is a more recent synthesis.
2. As well as the genetic code DNA, according to R. Jakobson and F. Jacob: see R. Jakobson and L. R. Waugh (i.p., first chapter). For a contrary view, see the remarks of J. Piaget (1973:8).
3. In a remarkably insightful paper presented at the First International Congress on the Semiotics of Art (Ann Arbor, Michigan, May 1978), Dr. Dora Vallier of Paris proposes a compatible distinction, termed 'plein et vide' (unpublished as of this writing).
4. The relationships here are consequently *asymmetric*, for under normal conditions there do not exist 'space forms' which are 'opaque', although there may very well be

conditions under which otherwise identical formations *significatively* contrast on the basis of lightness and darkness.

5. In the linguistic code, the situation is evidently the case that there may exist phonemic units which manifest distinctive features of (+consonantalism, +vocalism)–e.g. the so-called liquids, as well as phonemics units which are (-consonantal, -vocalic)– e.g. so-called glides, according to Jakobson: see Jakobson and Waugh (i.p.), for the most recent analysis. Such a situation may be correlative to the noncoterminosity of space/mass and transparency/opacity in the architectonic system. In both codes, of course, the situation is code- and context-specific.

6. The subject of the binarily-opposed nature of color perception is a complicated one, lucidly discussed by Zollinger and others, and reported from a comparative point of view by Jakobson and Waugh (i.p.) with regard to the phenomena of 'colored hearing' and synaesthesia. See also the discussions of color perception in J. Hochberg (1972).

7. A detailed examination of architectonic matrixing will be found in D. Preziosi (1979a, Chapter III), with reference to Minoan domestic contexts.

8. See above, n. 7.

9. In other words, it appears to be the case, in the development of semiosis in the human line, that there is a progression from less densely sense-determinative signing to more densely sense-determinative signing. If this is indeed the case, it would invert the impression that the development of human semiotic systems proceeds from states wherein double articulation is minimal to states in which it is maximal (i.e. toward states in which singularity of reference is minimal). Such an inversion would induce a fundamental change in our notions of 'architectural history', permitting what may turn out to be a more realistic picture of architectonic diachrony. For example, it is patent that in the history of a built environment in a given culture what may distinguish earlier from later formations may be the *density* of their polysemy: components of a formation which in an earlier state functioned principally in sense-discriminative ways may in a later state be employed sense-determinatively. Thus what for the Roman architect-theoretician Vitruvius is considered sense-determinative or directly significative in the componential organization of a Hellenic temple (e.g. the associations between particular column types and anthropomorphic categories) may originally have carried no such direct signification in their original contexts. In part this *drive toward polysemy* is augmented by a particular structural property of the architectonic code–namely, its (relative) object-permanence–and attests once again to the cumulative nature of architectonic (and semiotic) diachrony as against a purported linearity of evolution. See in this regard the recent volume by S. Giedion (1971); one of the most insightful discussions of the nature of 'time' in artifactual diachrony remains G. Kubler (1965). A provisional model of the mechanics of cumulative diachrony and polysemy is given in a student paper of mine published under the title 'Cessavit deinde ars', in the *Athens Journal*, 1966. It is patent that in the appropriation of a house, aspects of its formation which initially were perceived in sense-discriminative ways tend, over time, toward sense-determination or direct signification, until eventually everything about a house becomes 'home'. This cumulative polysemy in the usage of built environments has seldom been examined in a systemetic fashion. The entire question is closely bound up with the nature of iconic symbolism, as saliently discussed by O. Jespersen in 1922 in his *Language: Its Nature, Development and Origins*, who notes that the iconic/symbolic import of sounds becomes *more* wide-spread in more *recent* stages of human languages. Such observed tendencies stand as an important critique of the

simplistic evolutionism implicit in the arguments of W. Fairservis regarding architecture and settlement organization, discussed in detail in Chapter V below.

10. The question as to whether the *figure* is the minimal sense-determinative unit in the hierarchy remains open. At this point it seems necessary to refer to the existence of *semantic features* of some type—*viz.* attributes of formation which are minimally directly-significative—in a manner correlative to distinctive features in its hierarchy. That there exist in the architectonic code such features is patent: indeed, we may suggest that there will be found to exist an entire network of such semantic features, comprising a domain of sign-types in its own right. This may be adduced on the basis of features of direct signification which perceptually cue certain meanings— e.g. features of a *configurative* nature which signal impending connectivities among *forms*, or which cue the perception of meaningful disjunctions among *forms* or *cells*. It should be clearly borne in mind that the notion of the *cell* is not coterminous with the colloquial notion of the 'room', for more than one *cell* (understood as a topological/behavioral unicum) may 'occupy' a single mass-bounded space (room). Such episodic zonings may be cued by a very wide variety of physical means, from changes in coloration, articulation of wall and floor surfaces, orientations and alignments of supportive infrastructures (furniture, artifacts, etc.);—i.e. in any number of ways besides 'walls' or mass-partitions. That such is the case is clearly illustrated by the formative organization of the unicameral Atoni house in Indonesian Timor, as discussed by C. Cunningham (1964: 34-68), where *cells* are contrasted syntagmatically by means of contrasts in size and orientation of platforms. A similar case may be seen in the organization of the house-unit at Catal Huyuk in early Neolithic Anatolia (Mellaart, 1964), and, indeed, in nearly every corpus.

It also seems evident that such *semantic features* may, depending upon code-specific circumstances, be encoded in binary or gradient fashion. Moreover, it may be the case that an attribute of formation may function both distinctively and determinatively: the same properties may, in a given code, cue both sense-discriminative and sense-determinative meanings. Clearly, the raised curb of a sidewalk functions in both ways—i.e. to cue the perception of differences in formation *per se*, as well as to cue the perception of different functional zones—i.e. *cells* with direct significations. Such a situation is correlative to that evident in linguistic codes, where a given distinctive feature (e.g. nasality) may function in directly-significative ways under certain conditions—as where its presence may also cue the expressive or physiognomic attributes of given speakers. In addition to distinctive features, linguists have pointed to the existence of sense-determinative attributes of formation, such as configurative, redundant, expressive, and physiognomic features (Jakobson and Waugh, i.p.). Certain of these features may be encoded in binary fashion, while others are encoded in a not-necessarily-binary fashion.

Hence we may expect to find correlative properties in the architectonic code, on comparative grounds as well as on the basis of internal evidence. We may consequently point to the *figure* as a sign-type composed of syntagmatically-simultaneous clusters of (one or more) *semantic features*, in a manner systemically-correlative to the internal situation on the sense-discriminative side, wherein *forms* are equivalently structured as *signantia*.

It is patent that architectonic *semantic features* will include attributes of formation of which some may also function distinctively, as well as those which have no discriminative function. In the same code, certain color-contrasts may function both ways, while others of essentially the same 'objective' nature may only function one of these ways: see D. Preziosi (1979a; Chapter I). The hierarchical network of architectonic signs, then, may be portrayed in its (provisional) fullness as follows:

distinctive features
forms
templates
. . . .
semantic features
cells
. . . .
matrices
(etc.)

It is on the horizon of the semantic features that much important work remains to be done—both in built environments and in verbal languages, not to speak of more broadly in cultural systems—for example in kinship—where to date the concept of the semantic feature has been approached, by and large, in a formalistic and mechanistic manner (e.g. '+male, +adult, +human', vs. '+female, +adult, +human', etc.); see in this regard, G. Leech (1974; Chapters 6 and 7). For a profoundly insightful discussion of semantic features in verbal language, see the work of C. H. van Schooneveld, reported in *Semiotic Transmutations*, 1978. In the author's view, the set of semantic features comprises an ordered and recursive hierarchical network.

One factor which induces a certain complexity into the whole situation is the phenomenon of *markedness*, which implicates an inherent *asymmetry* in all discussions of semantic oppositions, whether architectonic, linguistic, or cultural. All choices of a binary nature in any semiotic code are not choices among covalents or equals, but choices between weighted or marked pairs. Here, as throughout the semiotic enterprise, our perspective will be most productive when grounded in a (truly) *relational* framework. For a lucid discussion of the nature of markedness in language and culture, see L. R. Waugh (i.p.).

5

Architectonic Evolution

PHYLOGENY AND ONTOGENY

Practically from the moment of birth, the newborn infant is engaged in interactional synchrony with his environment. He is not passively tracking environmental events; he is, in fact, engaged in a cognitive and perceptual 'dance' with objects and people.[1]

However a child learns his language—or his culture— it is clear that the process does not involve opening one's eyes with the effect that in a flash all the relative clauses of English or the tone patterns of Chinese immediately light up in the brain, once the child realizes where he is.[2]

Children simulate, piece together and construct a real world and its contents over time—over an extended period of time lasting many years. This process never reaches closure in any absolute sense, for it is clear that a culture is not a closed or well-formed system, not a finite block of information, not a limited set of resources.

Ontogenetic development is an extended, complex, and dynamic set of processes which it may be convenient, from an analytic perspective, to represent as a dynamically equilibrated series of conceptual thresholds or stages of development. Certain kinds of operant behavior may be taken as indices of the assimilation of various kinds of concepts ('object permanence', the principle of the conversation of liquids, etc.).[3]

It may be useful to represent the phylogenetic development of the species in a similar fashion, as a transform of ontogenetic development in some sense. The picture of cultural and cognitive phylogenesis may be constructed upon similar indices in the sense that certain kinds of artifactual evidence may purport to reveal certain stages in cognitive sophistication.

Thus, the presence in the fossil record of tools which serve to make other tools can be seen as a conceptual advance relative to simple appropriation of environmental objects as tools for individual purposes. In the fossil record, it is evident that the former postdates the latter. But the former does not *replace* the latter; in a subsequent archaeological horizon, the two activities coexist. Cultural phylogeny and individual ontogeny are, in a number of complex ways, cumulative, and in this sense may reveal a certain correlativity of process.

But whether cultural phylogenesis *mirrors* neonate ontogenesis (or vice versa) is an open, and vexed, question.

Certainly in one sense this *cannot* be so: it seems most unlikely that an adult humanoid of 300,000 B.P. possessed a level of maturity in (e.g.) space-conception equivalent to that of a contemporary five year old. In other words, if it is the case (as evidently it is) that in contemporary neonates topological space-conception emerges prior to metric-geometric conceptualization,[4] this cannot imply that a Pleistocene ancestor of twenty-five years of age would be at a level of conceptualization of spatial relations equivalent to our own five year old.

Obviously, such a twenty-five year old would be a biosocial failure; he would not be able to behave spatially in personally and socially useful ways. Moreover, he would be inferior to a young chimpanzee who can navigate a highly complex arboreal web with ease and confidence.

Not a few models of cultural phylogenesis have incorporated similarly absurd assumptions, however well-hidden. Moreover, a number of otherwise well-intentioned studies in an architectonic framework have been built upon equally flimsy half-hidden foundations.[5] Indeed, there is a long tradition of this in the history of architectural (and art) history.

Few discussions of the question of architectonic evolution have been as patently recapitulative as that recently put forth by W. Fairservis in his 1975 study of settlement organization as an index of cognitive development.[6] In the present chapter, we will address the issues raised by this writer, as well as, more briefly, those raised in a similar vein by the anthropologist A. Marshack in his analyses of Paleolithic figurative art.[7]

It has never been entirely clear what 'primitiveness' in the architectonic—or indeed in the artifactual—realm really should mean.

It *cannot* be equated with greater or lesser technological ability in the construction of architectonic formations—i.e. in the material realization of architectonic signs. Nor can it be substantiated that certain kinds of formal typologies are necessarily earlier or later than others: there is no evidence for a chronological primacy of curvilinear vs. rectilinear construction.[8] Nor is it entirely clear that primitiveness is necessarily to be equated with simplicity (vs. complexity) of formal structural organization.

Such assumptions are based on a false picture of architectonic organization which held that a code is necessarily (1) grounded in particular object-types, and (2) based on 'regularized' geometricality. It is also grounded (3) in a mechanistic or machine view of architectonic objects (the engineering fallacy) which confuses technological complexity with architectonic sophistication. A house is not a 'machine for living' but a system for the production of meaning by its user(s).

We might as well claim that a language with an eight-case nominal system is more sophisticated than one with three, or that a language whose speech-acts have been recorded on magnetic tape is more advanced than one spoken by an isolated group of individuals in the Amazon, never heard or recorded by outsiders.

An architectonic system realized in animal skins supported on bamboo poles is in no way more *conceptually* primitive than one realized in concrete and glass. In part the confusion stems from received art-historical theory wherein the material realizations of architectonic signs are confused with the signs themselves. A pyramid is not *per se* a conceptually more advanced architectonic formation than a 'simple' reed hut or a pile of stones placed as a cairn over the remains of an individual, even if the former may differ from the latter in the same society in terms of the diversity and complexity of its associated semantic domains, or the multidimensionality of its referents. But the latter is culture and code-specific, and the formative 'simplicity' or complexity of an object is not inherently iconic with respect to the simplicity or complexity of its associations. Nor would anyone claim that polysyllabic words are more semantically complex than monosyllabic words as signs.

As we have seen above, an architectonic sign is a combination of a formation and a referent; the formation (that-which-signifies) is realized or represented materially (it has, in Peirceian terms, a 'ground').[9] The material system of an architectonic code is itself a highly complex system, ancillary to the organization of the code itself, and reflective of an extraordinary variety of extra- and para-architectonic constraints, dependent for the most part upon available resources in an ecology as socioculturally perceived. It is quite unique in this respect, having no directly-comparable analog in other semiotic codes (particularly vocal language).

The confusions alluded to above partly stem from a skewed or ambiguous focus with respect to the architectonic system's order *per se*. Furthermore, it would be patently simplistic and mechanistic to refer to the relationships between an architectonic code and its systems of material realization as directly equivalent to the 'deep' vs. 'surface' structure of once current models of linguistic semiosis: the fact that the architectonic code is realized in any conceivable set of ecological resources addressed to the optical channel induces a unique complexity into the system, quite unlike what is available to us as speakers.

In fact, apparent differences in architectonic sophistication among the multitude of systems presently extant are an artifact of a misunderstanding of the nature of the architectonic medium itself. Despite enormous differences in the use of materials or in the ability (or disability) to span great distances in a single bound, the simple fact is that there is a fundamental family resemblance among all the extant and recently-extant built environments known. This conceptual homology extends to settlement systems back to the origins of more or less permanent cities less than a dozen millenia ago. Nor can it be demonstrated that the settlement systems of contemporary hunter-gatherers and various migratory societies are in any fundamental sense less sophisticated than the less ephemeral environments of their megalopolitan cousins.[10]

As we have seen above, one of the features of architectonic systems is, in addition to their alternative material realizations, the disposability and interchangeability of those formations (within code-specific constraints), as well as their variable permanence and potential mobility.

W. Fairservis has recently argued (Fairservis 1975:13-54) that the organization of various settlements in the Paleolithic and early Neolithic periods provides evidence for increasing cognitive sophistication in the early human line. He sees the organization of three 'key' settlements as representing different stages in human cognitive evolution paralleling stages in the phylogenetic development of contemporary individuals.

He regards the settlement at Terra Amata at Nice in southern France, for example, as representative of an 'enactive' stage of cognitive evolution, contrasting this site, dated to about 300,000 B.P., with the site of Dolni Vestonice in Czechoslovakia (datable to about 25,000 B.P.), which is said to represent an 'ikonic' stage of evolution. Both are contrasted to the site of Catal Huyuk in south central Turkey, inhabited as early as eight millennia ago, which is said to represent a 'symbolic' stage in conceptual development. These three stages—enactive, ikonic, and symbolic—are taken directly from the three levels of phylogenetic conceptual growth proposed by J. Bruner and others (Bruner 1966), whose validity *in se*, however, is not the subject of our attention here.

Fairservis' views are posited in part on the assumption that the records of a built environment of a nonextant society are 'readable' within certain reasonable limits. In general, we shall not question this assumption *per se*, and it partakes of a number of basic assumptions of the branch of epistemology known as archaeology itself, whose activities comprise a complexly-cross-indexed set of inferences regarding the nature of adequate evidence.[11]

The problem, however, concerns the *necessary* nature of the writer's *signata (viz.*, the stages of development). In the first place, there is the problematic application of patterns of development drawn from a different realm—the given metaphor or model—whose usefulness is ultimately analogical rather than inherently iconic. The author patently takes a given process—the stages of cognitive development in the contemporary child—and in effect says 'what if the evolution of built environments (or cultures) were analogous to the conceptual growth of an individual; what kind of evidence would be required to make a reasonable case for such an evolution?'

The 'kind of evidence' found is represented by three key sites between 300,000 B.P. and 8,000 B.P. with what the author sees as significantly contrastive, formative features.

Such hypothesizing is not only not uncommon; it may be useful, yielding insights into signification often not easily had from other perspectives. Understanding proceeds and grows in any number of alternative ways, within and without formalized paradigms. This is not the problem. A given model or paradigm exists within a context of proximate and ultimate uses and functions. It may be useful for certain purposes to simulate the evolution of material culture with a model abstracted from the apparent processes in the growth of a plant, or of a mathematical formalism.

The problem with Fairservis' hypothetical model is twofold. The first concerns the usefulness of a recapitulative model wherein the growth of a culture or of a species is taken to be a transitive transformation of the growth of an individual. For a variety of reasons this cannot have been literally the case. But it may be useful to *force* such an analogy in the hope of at least highlighting the question on the basis of how and why such a literal model will fail, thereby learning something about how to re-ask a useful question.

Fairservis' study, however, evidently takes its probe seriously as a probe or model, and on these grounds we are forced to take issue with it.

The second problem is in a sense more important, and involves a number of hidden assumptions and patent misunderstandings. This concerns the nature of the evidence itself and the author's conception of it. He replicates the confusion referred to above concerning technological ability (the engineering fallacy), leaving the reader to surmise that 'less-well-made' architectonic formations, and, presumably, more 'irregular' geometric organizations manifest in such objects, are direct indexes of conceptual immaturity or primitiveness.

In other words, the author would have us believe that the *signantia* of material culture are necessarily directly related to their *signata* in an iconic (vs. 'ikonic')[12] manner, which is patently false.

Furthermore, Fairservis' assessment of the formative evidence (more strictly speaking, however, his 'data' are 'capta') is grounded in a misapprehension of the inherent variability, interchangability and disposability of architectonic materializations, and on the nature of the 'medium' itself. It would appear that his arguments are grounded in a further fallacy, wherein an architectonic formation is seen as the 'record' of a significative transmission, rather than a component of that transmission, as a component of a sign. He might as well argue that old Egyptian is a more primitive language than modern English because the former is recorded hieroglyphically while the latter is recorded alphabetically.[13] An architectonic system is *not* a system of forms but a system of *relationships*.

The fact that written language and built environments generically addresses the same *sensory* channels does not mean that the latter is merely another kind of visual text or record; this should be clear from our discussions above. (Nor for that matter can it be seriously claimed that architectonic formations are clever chromatic and sculptural transmutations of lexical items.)

There is nothing whatsoever about the organization of the three built environments central to the author's argument which is conceptually different from those around us.

Furthermore, it is unclear in Fairservis' presentation whether or not the particular architectonic formations discussed are themselves to be taken as 'enactive', 'ikonic', or 'symbolic' artifacts. What would an 'enactive' hut look like? Did the inhabitants of Dolni Vestonice speak an 'ikonic' language?

Until we are able to more fully understand the nature of architectonic semiosis, it would be unwise to take the evidence of architectonic formations as providing *direct* indices of a society's world view and its conceptual sophistication *vis-a-vis* other societies.

Necessarily, a built environment is a spatial locus which 'contains' (in a variety of senses) at least part of a group's total repertoire of activities. Much of what is extant at a site is a function of differing situations, purposes, activities, and the amount of time that site has been occupied. The longer the period of occupation, the greater and more varied will be the activities that occur there.[14] The latter may or may not be reflected in the amount of complexity of the extant materials. Few of these factors are related to each other in a direct, proportional, or one-to-one fashion: they are necessarily indirect—i.e. metonymic and metaphoric.

This raises serious problems in the attempt to compare one site with another. Large inter-site differences may indicate less than one might suppose. We would concur with J. Yellen who, in his 1977 ethnoarchaeological study of the !Kung (Yellen 1977:132-136), suggests that an analytic scale ranging from simple to complex may in the long run prove more useful than a classificatory approach which posits aprioristic categories.

As far as possible, however, it is necessary to be as explicit as we can about our basic assumptions and the purposes which an analytic perspective are to be put. Notions of simplicity and complexity are themselves culturally shaped.

The emphasis on the nature of architectonic semiosis in the present study is based upon the writer's view that in order to understand *what* an architectonic object might signify (within our own societies or in the Pleistocene), we need to understand *how* such formations signify, based upon a careful and comprehensive analysis of actual built environments in the daily life of a group. In trying to understand anything as complex as the evolution of built environments in human history, we need to be conversant with architectonic systems themselves.

A built environment—whether an urban agglomerate or a seasonal or daily encampment—contains and broadcasts information about the social and cognitive world of a people. An architectonic formation provides evidence for the state of a society at a certain time and place. But it is not always clear what is being signified or how a given formation is signifying. Nor is it necessarily clear that the analyst's sense of what the signifiers themselves are is not a projection of assumptions based on his own cultural experience: the boundaries or closures upon significative unities are themselves code-specific.

In other words, it is not always clear what the 'formations' themselves are. Often it is only through long experience derived from cross-systemic study that an analyst will begin to know what to look for, coupled with the application of reasonably adequate theoretical parameters.

Faced with two contiguous settlements with sharply contrastive formations, the experience he brings to bear upon a comparative study must be able to tell him that one is a summer camp and the other a winter camp of the same group rather than the settlements of two distinct groups.

He cannot automatically assume that two isomorphic formations necessarily signify identical things or indicate the same range
of conceptual association. Hut J at site X may in fact be very
nearly identical to hut K at Y, but the former may be a dwelling,
the latter a symbol of the solidarity of a family group whose dwelling focus is a nearby hearth. An indication of the situation faced
by the archaeologist or ethnographer is clearly given by Yellen's
description of the !Kung hut:

Hut forms vary according to the season in which the hut is constructed and
the length of time it is expected to be occupied. During the rainy season, huts
tend to be substantial and well thatched, as are huts near permanent water-
holes, which are occupied for several consecutive months. Conversely, non-
rainy-season, temporary huts tend to be of much more flimsy construction
and at times may be considered 'symbolic' at best. Generally, each nuclear
family builds a hut, as do unmarried adults, widows, and widowers, the structures providing not only some protection from the rain but also very wel-
come shade during the heat of the day, as well as a private place for storing
belongings. Rainy season huts are circular, with a domed roof, and measure
up to 2 meters in diameter as well as height. A hut can be constructed in
several hours by a husband and wife. . . . Dry season, temporary huts are less
substantial, and may be placed so as to incorporate living vegetation as
'walls'. They often lack roofs, sometimes form only a half circle, and usually
are not thatched. Their major functions are to demarcate a private family
area and provide shade. Very few activities take place inside the hut itself.
Children sometimes construct small play huts (Yellen 1977:143-144).

Even in a society with such an 'ephemeral' built environment,
the amount of formative and significative variety is very great indeed. Here we find material, formal and functional variation as
well as differences in the nature of the associations between a formation and its referent(s). The differences between rainy and non-
rainy season huts is more than material or technological in this
case: it is *formal.*

Yellen's study attempts to indicate how the careful study of
ethnographic material may provide sounder bases for the archaeological reconstruction of human environments, and how, conversely, the archaeologist's long-range view can cast ancillary perspectives on the ethnographic present. His work reflects a growing
and intensive interest in the relationships between archaeology and
ethnography which promise increased illumination of the Paleolithic past (Yellen 1977:xi).

The study of architectonic semiosis in its focus upon origins and evolution intercepts the aforementioned relationship in a perpendicular fashion, providing an additional input into these questions insofar as it seeks to systematically understand the nature of signification in a variety of media. Conversely, ethnography and archaeology will offer the indispensible data for the elaboration of an adequate and realistic semiotics, which, if it is not to fly away like many of the formalistic balloons of recent generative semantics, must be so grounded.

In short, a reasonable picture of the emergence and evolution of human culture must incorporate a realistic sense not only of social communication in general, but in particular (because fossil traces of built environments provide the archaeologist with primary datum) an adequate understanding of architectonic systems. Even when functioning as a 'stage set' for social behavior, the built environment is a member of the cast.

The thesis put forward by Fairservis is unacceptable, essentially, on three grounds. First, it represents a dubious application of ontogenetic processes to phylogenetic evolution. Second, it misunderstands the complex ways in which artifactual systems signify. Finally, the architectonic evidence (at least) would not support his fundamental thesis (assuming the latter itself were unquestionable, which it is not), for there is nothing about the settlement remains discussed which is in any way significantly different from our own formations.

If it is in fact the case that there is a fundamental conceptual homology between the former and the latter, then there is no evidence for a conceptual evolution in the architectonic system itself during the past third of a million years.

The question which is most salient here, of course, is whether or not the proposed homology can be supported. There are a number of important problems, one of which is that the remains of the Terra Amata site suggest an association with *homo erectus* (or possibly *homo Neanderthalensis*) rather than *homo sapiens* (Fairservis 1975:55-59), on the basis of the nature of the artifacts and debris. The human remains found at Dolni Vestonice a quarter of a million years ago are clearly *sapiens*.

TERRA AMATA

Terra Amata was a seasonal camp along the Mediterranean littoral, occupied perhaps in late spring and summer undoubtedly in order to exploit the food resources of the shoreline. The camp was occupied for about twenty years, the chief artifact being an ovoid hut which fell into ruins after each yearly occupation; the remains were covered over each year and a new hut built over the remains, superimposing a new hut floor precisely over the previous one, suggesting that it was the same band which returned each year (Figure 1).

The hut itself varied slightly in size each year, within a limit of length of 26 to 49 feet, and from 13 to 20 feet in width. It was carefully constructed each time with a circumferential row of upright sticks bent slightly inward so as to meet together at top. The stick foundations were reinforced on their outer sides by a row of stones chosen to be of roughly equal size. Entrance was on one of the short sides, on the west.

Within were four centrally aligned large posts to support the ridge pole which evidently ran longitudinally, itself supporting the inwardly-inclined wall-poles. Most likely, the latter were interspersed and tied together along the ridge pole. Between the two innermost central posts was a hearth or fire-pit which was associated with a line of stones near its north side; the latter may have been a fire wind-break and/or a support structure for cooking utensils. Fragments of stones were found elsewhere inside the hut, evidently representing several loci for toolmaking activities.

The artifactual evidence apart from the hut itself and the remains of pebble and flake tools is scanty; there are some sticks of red ocher, and an imprint in the sand floor suggests the remains of a wooden bowl or dish.

The hut itself is a remarkable object, giving evidence of careful planning and construction involving the coordination of varied labors. The builders *knew* what they were doing, and the formation suggests a long history of constructional practice: it is not an experimental object. The wall is laid out in a very careful line and is made up of poles selected and trimmed to equal length and diameter. The circumferential retaining stones around the outer

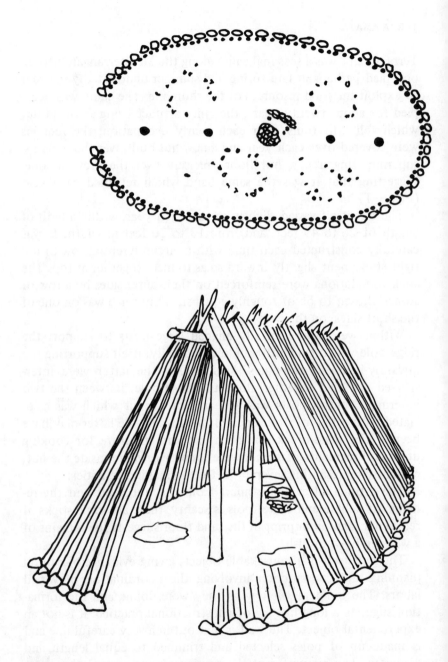

Figure 1.

side of the line of poles were chosen to be of equal size. The central four posts, also equal in size, are embedded in the ground at equal intervals, and the hearth occupies the very center of the room within the line of posts running east-west.

The hearth itself comprised a bed of pebbles forming a circular surface, possibly slightly below grade. The associated line of stones on its north side may have served as a windbreak or a support platform for skewers to cook game and seafood.

It is not known who lived in the huts; judging from their size, they may have been the yearly stations of a band or extended family. The structure appears to have been a combined dwelling, kitchen, and workspace; in other words, a multifunctional locus of activity. Since there was more than one locus of toolmaking activities within (judging from the groups of debris), it may be that each man made his own tool kit, and it may be that his activities were in the service of himself and his immediate relatives. The social organization of the Terra Amatans is unknown, but the artifactual remains suggest a number of possible pictures of organization which are not unfamiliar, on comparative grounds.

The architectonic organization of the hut is also not unfamiliar. It is not a random collection of loci, an arbitrary aggregate loosely bound by an arbitrary border; it is a complex object whose component parts are designed to interact in a fully integrated way. Each formation, in other words, reflects and is modified by the presence of the others. It is, in fact, a system, a built *environment*, which is designed to function in concert with other seasonal environments elsewhere.

If the picture of !Kung settlement described above may be taken as a reasonable guide, then this warm-season formation would have existed alongside cold-weather quarters away from the exposed seashore. The present structure is very well suited to its situation, providing at the same time needed shade from the sun along the beach as well as a certain draftiness of construction to allow for interior cooling. We may imagine that the winter quarters of the people were more substantial in construction, perhaps also notably different in geometric organization.

Each year the Terra Amatans returned to precisely the same spot on this beach. The place may have been *marked* by the remains of the previous year's hut, or, if the latter were covered over before last year's departure, by some indexical sign such as an upright stick or pile of stones.

It is not known why the group stopped coming here after twenty years, nor is it known where they built before that.

The nature of the hut at Terra Amata is in no way fundamentally different from the constructions of contemporary hunter-gatherers in its conceptual organization, as observed by Leakey in connection with his observations of the G/wi (Leakey and Lewin 1977:129, 167). Its existence attests to a tradition in building, although we have at present no evidence for how old such a tradition might have been, whether only a few generations or many millennia. Judging from the fact that the nature of the material culture represented at Terra Amata appears to have remained relatively constant for another quarter of a million years, we may surmise that the architectonic tradition was itself similarly stable during that time, and that such stability may also have extended for a long time before the appearance of Terra Amata itself.

The existence of an architectonic object of the level of sophistication exhibited by this hut *should* attest to a fair degree of advancement in verbal language itself, but it is not at all clear what kind of correlations might be evidenced. In effect, we need to know much more about the daily-life interactive usages of verbal and visual communication in general, and we need to explore this phenomenon more thoroughly in the ethnographic record.

This is not simply a matter of generic correlation of architectonic component formations with purported lexical vocabulary. It is clear both on ethnographic and theoretical grounds that the two systems are semiautonomous, although it is unclear to what extent this may have *always* been so.

We need to know *what kind* of linguistic parastructure would be required for the generation of symbolic artifacts of this type. It is unclear whether such an architectonic object could exist in concert with a spoken language which did not have the same generic range of 'design features'[15] as our own languages.

The writer is of the opinion that a correlatively-designed vocal language, with duality of patterning, phonemic organization, displacement, conventionality, and so forth, would have been present, but there is no direct and secure evidence for such a claim.

To be sure, the complexity of the *distinctions* among the various component members of the Terra Amata hut, and the implied need for cooperative planning and integrated construction suggests equivalent linguistic subtlety and complexity, a carefully-calibrated sense of sameness and difference (and sameness *in* difference). This is not to imply necessarily that there need have been a direct one-on-one correlation between component architectonic distinctions and lexico-semantic distinctions. Construction of this type would seem to suggest evidence for abilities in counting and the representation of material quantities, but this need not have been independently 'vocalizable' verbally.

A desire for collecting stones of identical size or sticks of two size-classes may be communicated quite easily nonverbally, or with minimum and ancillary vocalization. But it seems to the present writer rather unlikely that the intelligence of the inhabitants of the site was not roughly equivalent cross-modally.

At any rate, the existence of this remarkable formation at such an early period cannot be securely taken as either a *terminus post quem* or a *terminus ante quem* for the emergence of the linguistic code as we know it today. To be sure, the ecological situation of the Terra Amatans with respect to the availability of scores of food sources, both marine and terrestrial, might also be linked with an extensive vocabulary on the linguistic side for the representation and communication of such information socially. But it is patently unclear what kind of *systemic* organization that vocabulary might have had. As we have stated, we feel it unlikely that the system of verbal language could have been conceptually much less sophisticated than the architectonic system itself.

But this cannot be proven given the state of our evidence. It is in such an area that Yellen's suggestions as to the importance of ethnographic analysis for illuminating the archeological record comes to the forefront: quite simply, we need to know what kind of linguistic parastructures are necessary to the generation of complex architectonic formations of this type, and intensive and systematic study of cross-modal semiosis in daily life becomes crucially important. We need, in short, a more complete picture of cross-modal *constructional* activity quite apart from the normal interactive usages of verbal and visual systems in completed contexts.

We will return to this generic question again in Chapter VI below. In contrast to a view that human culture achieved a 'symbolic' level of development only toward the latter stages of the Paleolithic, there exists an increasing body of evidence for symbolic behavior in artifacts of the period of Terra Amata, in association with the Acheulian period of a *homo erectus* who was developing toward being *homo sapiens*.

PALEOLITHIC SYMBOLISM

Artifacts of evidently 'symbolic' character have been turning up in recent years in surprisingly early contexts. Such artifacts antedate the familiar figurative 'art' of the Aurignacian period by scores of millennia. Since the late 1960s, detailed microscopic analyses of shaped and engraved objects have begun to reveal a picture of the conceptual advancement and sophistication of our ancestors in the early human line beyond what would have been admitted a mere decade or two ago.[16]

These 'abstract' images, whatever their contextual associations or referential usages, appear to reveal, in the processes of their generation, not only a fine coordination and focus of hand, eye and brain, but 'a cognitive capacity and competence for abstraction, modeling, and manufacture of a different order than that which can be deduced from the subsistence tool industries', according to A. Marshack (1976:307).

Although this competence involved a use of hands and tools, it may well also be allied to linguistic competence as well as toolmaking. The engraved images of this period suggest a phenomenological reference, documenting an awareness of the natural world in a variety of different ways. Marschack sees the manufacture of these symbolic images as providing important evidence for the emergence of complex cultural capacities:

In the manufacture of a Mousterian symbolic image, one hand (presumably the right, in most cases) held the cutting tool and shaped the image. The other hand held the material being worked, adjusting it for orientation and judging weight, size, hardness, pressure, and so on. The right hand was forming a particular class of image in what might be termed a 'specifying' activity, which, though nonlinguistic, was related to 'naming'.

It was not merely the manipulative capacity of the hominid hand as tool user that was involved, but a two-handed competence with a highly evolved right-handed, vision-oriented specialization for symbol forming, aided by a left hand supplying a different input. This, of course, has relevance for lateralization, cerebral dominance, *cross-modal association*, and so on, but involved also are such 'modes' or aspects as motivation, plans, cognitive modelling, symbolic sequencing, and an exceedingly fine acuity in the kinesthetic, somesthetic and visual inputs. Above and behind these testable skills there is the more generalized capacity to create and to function within long-term, artificial (or cultural) *'equations of relevance* (italics D. P.) (Marshack 1976:307).

Marshack goes on to suggest that the use of symbolic images required some form of spoken language to maintain and explain the tradition, and adds that we need to examine the possibility that visually oriented two-handedness of the human type, with all of its cross-modal neurological correlates, evolved *in conjunction with* an increasingly lateralized, corticalized capacity for vocal communication.

It will be recalled that our examination of the design features and functions of the architectonic code as a system of visual semiosis suggested a similar scenario for ontogenetic development. We would concur with Marshack's emphasis on cross-modal associability and functional 'equations of relevance' (cf.: 'relational invariance').

Furthermore, he points to the 'culture complex' *as a whole* (and not just one or another key activity such as toolmaking or hunting) as providing the environmental matrix and selective pressure:

With an increasing complexity in hominid cultures there would be need for an increased capacity of *variable marking both in the visual and the vocal modes*. This would be due in part to the increasing variability and the concurrent *culturalization of objects, processes, actions, and relations* (italics D. P.) (Marshack 1976:309).

He states further that

... the symbolic images of the Mousterian and Upper Palaeolithic could probably be 'named' and the meaning and usage of any one image could perhaps be explained. But the use of such artificial images *was itself a mode* and an 'equation of relevance', one that had to be learned and yet could not be linguistically explained. Human languages, like human image systems, function only in devised contexts. The search for language origins, therefore, should be directed toward the complex nature of the evolving, generalizing hominid capacity for artificial, cultural modelling and symbolic structuring *in all modes* (italics D.P.) (Marshack 1976:310).

Such a general picture of phylogenesis is homologous to that which we have proposed to be *required* on the basis of the internal organization and design features of the architectonic code itself, as we currently know it, and on its characteristic properties of multimodal associability and address—a situation, moreover, reflected in verbal language itself.[17]

The inherent multifunctionality of contemporary semiotic systems, in concert with the varied nature of architectonic and linguistic sign-types (for example, of indexical, iconic and symbolic orientations) has suggested a model of interactive, cross-modal, coalescent emergence and ontogenesis of the built environment compatible with the spirit of Marshack's generic model.

It is evident, for example, that his focus upon the 'symbolic' function recalls features of our 'aesthetic' orientation in artifactual semiosis, and he aptly distinguishes between the 'use' or 'meaning' of the engraved images (our referential or context-oriented function) and the evidence they provide for symbolic purposes.

It is clear that evidence for symbolic signing at such an 'early' period does not simply push back Fairservis' ontogenetic model to a yet more distant horizon. Instead, it turns it both upside-down and inside-out. The relative 'lateness' of 'iconic' signing (assuming the fossil record to be directly reflective of the actual state of affairs) in the figurative 'art' of the later Paleolithic would seem to partly reverse Fairservis' sequence, while the evidence for cross-modal association and multifunctionality of signs puts the picture of ontogenesis into a different perspective. It suggests to the present writer a coalescent emergence of increasingly cross-indexed and palimpsested systems, resulting in a fully integrated system of social communication, expression, and representation.

We do not know if this coalescence occurred rapidly or slowly; the fossil record is too fragmentary to attest to either picture.

Our understanding of social communication is undergoing a shift in orientation and focus at the present time wherein more attention is being given the total communicative event in all its complex multimodality. In large part, this new emphasis is the result of an increased understanding of human cognitive processes themselves. We will briefly address these issues in the next chapter.

NOTES

1. See T. G. R. Bower (1977:30 f.).
2. This observation is from a conversation with D. L. Bolinger.
3. See in this regard the work of Jean Piaget and his associates, and in particular J. Piaget (1954, 1955).
4. See J. Piaget (1970b:30 ff.; 1978).
5. For a discussion of the subject in a traditional art-historical framework, see J. Rykwert (1976).
6. See W. Fairservis (1975).
7. See A. Marshack (1972a, 1972b, 1976).
8. That is to say, arguments referring to the supposed technological ease of constructing architectonic formations of a curvilinear nature are patently absurd; equally unsupportable are arguments which imply that such constructions are *symbolically* more primitive or fundamental.
9. An excellent discussion of Peirceian semiotics may be found in the writings of David Savan: see in particular Savan 1976; see also references to the work of Peirce in the writings of R. Jakobson (1977, Chapter II, n. 20), and the important discussions by Umberto Eco in his *A Theory of Semiotics* (1977).
10. See J. Yellen (1977). On the fallacy of technological/physical determinism, see C. Norberg-Schulz (1965:102); and A. Rapoport (1969, *passim*).
11. For an intelligent and sensible discussion of this question, see J. Yellen (1977) and below, Chapter VI.
12. W. Fairservis (1978:39-54, 74-118). On 'iconism' in architectonic systems, see D. Preziosi (1979a, Chapter IV), and the interesting work of M. Wallis (1975), particularly Chapter 4, 'Semantic and Symbolic Elements in Architecture: Iconology as a First Step towards an Architectural Semiotic', pp. 39-58, with extensive references.
13. On the origins of semiotic codes which function to endow verbal language with cross-modal object permanence, see the recent research of D. Schmandt Besserat (1977, Chapter I, n. 4).
14. See Yellen (1977:1-12), and recall our arguments in Chapter IV, note 9.
15. On design features, see our discussions above in Chapter IV, and Chapter II, n. 15.
16. See above, note 7, and N. Toporov, "Toward the Origin of Certain Poetic-Symbols: the Palaeolithic Period," in H. Baran, ed., *Semiotics and Structuralism: Readings from the Soviet Union*, 1976, pp. 184-225, for a discussion of markedness relations in Palaeolithic cave painting composition.
17. On multimodality in communication, see D. Preziosi (1978d, Appendix A) and M. Silverstein (1976).

6

Communication and Culture

SEMIOSIS AND COGNITIVE CAPACITY

This study has focussed upon the question of the origins and evolution of the built environment as a semiotic system from the perspectives of its organization as a system and its characteristic properties of multifunctionality and cross-modal address. We have attempted to relate these design features to artifactual and communicative behavior in the primate background and in the early human line.

Necessarily, this is only a part of the picture. We have only summarily discussed communicative behavior, in general, and have only suggestively embedded that behavior in the context of human perceptual and cognitive behavior.

Clearly, nonhuman creatures of amazingly different types have thus far managed to survive quite well, despite periodic extinctions induced by human radiation, without the complex artifactual modalities we are accustomed, in our parochialism, to view as necessary to social communication. The traditional emphases placed upon the formational peculiarities of human communication and representation has often resulted in an inability to understand and appreciate the ways in which other species perform isofunctional activities with other means.

But kangaroos only 'lack' language from a human perspective; they communicate vocally and somatically in ways quite adequate to their needs as kangaroos. The human sociocultural way of life represents an adaptive departure from a primate background which has become suitable and necessary for our own specific purposes. Dolphins have gone in different directions; however 'smart' they may be, they evidently do not need to build underwater cities, and it would be foolish to fault them for such a lack, however implicitly we might do so.

It is apparently the case that organisms do not necessarily possess equal cognitive capacities in all sensory modes. Intelligence appears to be mode-specific, even though some modes are closely interrelated, and a creature may not necessarily be able to demonstrate (to us) a cognitive capacity with its voice that it can express with its limbs or its nose. Even in human societies, different grades of visual or verbal intelligence are variously prized at different times.

The evolution of communicative capacity in the human line appears to be characterized by the development of increased abilities in all available sensory modalities,[1] although this is not uniform, as evidenced by our rudimentary olfactory system (relative to many other species).

But on the average, *homo sapiens* excels in virtually all communicative and representational modes. It would seem to be the case, as a number of writers have suggested,[2] that humans have evolved a capacity for cross-modal transfer resulting in a truly holistic or global organization of intelligence. Our sensory systems have become closely integrated and complexly cross-indexed.

The evolutionary processes of human multimodal signing and marking remains largely invisible to us. The collateral neurological developments which resulted in greater capacities in this direction in humans are in some sense related to the cumulative elaboration of complex cross-connections among those portions of the brain responsible for the processing of information in various sensory channels. It has been suggested[3] that in man the angular gyrus is the neural elaboration that was critical for the attachment of a 'name' or construct to a cross-modal percept,[4] resulting, as we have suggested above, in not one but several 'common codes'.

As noted before, the subject of cross-modal perception in humans (and others) has been receiving increasing attention in recent years. It has become more and more evident that a realistic picture of human semiosis must address the total communicative set in its cross-modal multifunctionality. Such a view is increasingly represented in the work of psychologists, linguists, primatologists, and biologists, for whom 'to separate communication from the overall information pickup and transmission capabilities of the individual would be a *tour de force* on the part of the human observer (Menzel and Johnson 1976:131).

Communication is, in general, a means to an end. A communicational system is a mechanism or instrument for solving the basic problems of coordinating and regulating an individual's society, discriminating each other's identity, age, sex, social background, group membership, emotional and motivational states, and the state of other objects and events in the environment, transmitting the capacity for similar accomplishments to progeny and others, securing thereby all of the requisites for survival and reproducttion.[5] Communication is embedded in the general perceptual and cognitive abilities of an organism, which have the primary features of being adaptive and purposeful.

It used to be common to propose a dichotomy between human and primate communication wherein the latter were seen only as communicating information about their internal emotional states, and as being unable to transmit information about objects in the environment.

In part, such a view was naive with respect to an understanding of the ways in which the latter type of information could be represented by a nonhuman primate. In addition, such a view was embedded in a narrow understanding of emotional and expressive behavior itself. As pointed out by A. Michotte (Michotte 1950), humans as well as other animals characteristically perceive 'emotion' as a modification of a signer's behavior in relation to oneself or in relation to some object or event. (In other words, as we have suggested above,[6] communication—both linguistic and architectonic—incorporates an emotive *function* as a particular kind of modificational *orientation* on one of the component parts of a transmission.) Communication is inherently multifunctional and multimodal.

That is to say, we judge the character and meaning of another being's internal state not merely from motor patterns and vocalizations, but also, and equally, from the *relationship* of these reactions to the rest of an environment: to a *context*.

A chimpanzee heads over in the direction of another giving loud 'food calls' not only because those calls might indicate how happy the signaler is, but because that internal state necessarily stands *in relation to* some environmental object or event. The particular 'call' anticipates the pervasive multifunctional orientation of human signs with its characteristic balancing of more than one orientation within varying degrees of dominance.

Not only must an organism be able to read and communicate information with regard to his conspecific fellows, it must also be able to 'read' the emotive and motivational states of other species who employ different systems of communication. We need to be able to fool enough of the trout for our purposes, just as the trout must be able to fool enough of us—or enough black bears—for its purposes. An organism will need to muster all of the perceptual systems it can to supply it with information necessary to its survival.

Communication is part of the general perceptual and cognitive activities of an organism. Particular signals or transmissions supplement and complement information available from other sources, including, most importantly, internal representational schemata and computational hypotheses.

A number of the received assumptions regarding animal communication are becoming increasingly untenable with the advance of comparative zoosemiotics—notably the assumption that there are indissoluble one-to-one correspondences between a signal and its referent(s), or the assumption that nearly all nonhuman communication patterns are entirely involuntary and nonintentional, or the assumption that object-reference or representation is a property of human semiosis alone.[7]

In part, of course, such assumptions have both dimly or clearly reflected a received 'territoriality' with respect to the preservation of particularly human characteristics, in contradistinction, on the one hand, to 'divinity' and, on the other hand, to 'animality', particularly in Western societies. One's identity is necessarily defined in relationship to other identities.

In fact, it is becoming clearer that many animals use a variety of different, partly redundant and interchaneable means for transmitting similar or isofunctional messages, revealing properties of paraphrase or transmutation formerly attributed to human communication alone. This is not to say that human communication is not unique in its power, flexibility, subtlety, and globality: it is, but these capacities did not rise full-blown in the minds of Adam, Eve, or Lilith. They have a history, however difficult it may be to read at present.

As we have seen in this study, the question of the origins and evolution of the built environment—and indeed of visual communication in general—can no longer be constrained to a consideration of formal and structural properties alone. We can only usefully advance our understanding within a broader *functional* framework whose appropriate analytic units will involve larger multimodal activities.

It has seem appropriate to suggest a model of architectonic communication wherein transmission can be most cogently understood in terms of orientations upon the component parts of a transmission which yield contrastive but coeval and integrated functions. An architectonic object can only be adequately understood as a formation wherein there is manifest a simultaneous bundling of varying functional orientations. These include, minimally, the referential address toward a context (incorporating the multiplicity of given usages), an addresser, an addressee, conation, contact, as well as the formation itself and the code itself, the latter two involving a difference in the range of focus.

All of these factors are code-specific to a large extent, and the search for architectonic universals (as for linguistic universals) must focus away from formal objecthood toward structure, function, purpose, and systemic signification. A continued focus upon a communicational system—whether architectonic or linguistic—within a simplistic machinelike metaphorical framework, can only cause us to see the component portions of communicational activity as discrete, apparently well-formed modules sequentially hooked up or plugged into each other.

The question of the origins and evolution of the built environment will not be resolved through the elaboration of formal typologies and their geneologies. Formational or object-types do not have a history except insofar as they provide *part* of the evidence for significative units—signs—which depend for their definition upon their multiple and dynamically-changing relationships to other signs of equivalent types. Forms have 'a life of their own' only in an indirect sense.

It is the *system itself* which should be focussed upon as a prime, as a totality upon which questions of adaptation and selection operate. However much the hut at Terra Amata may appear to tell us us of the state of human culture and cognition, it is clear that formation was a member of a network of formations—a corpus—which itself (if we had it before us) could begin to answer some of our questions. While it seems most unlikely on comparative and ethnographic grounds, it might have been the case that the Terra Amatans built identical huts, in identical sizes and orientations, under every ecological condition they encountered. We would then be dealing with an architectonic system of quite a different order from that of Dolni Vestonice a quarter of a million years later, where we find several different kinds of formations coexistant.

But it seems unlikely that *homo erectus* had an invariant response to any environment, given the nature of the formative organization of the Terra Amata hut itself. Despite appearances to untrained human eyes, even beehives vary in formation to accommodate different environmental conditions.

At any rate, our main point here is that a reasonably realistic assessment of the evolution of human culture as evidenced through architectonic artifacts can only emerge with a more complete picture of a group's built environment. And in addition we should remain clear that the simplicity or complexity (both formal and material) of a formation is no necessary index of the 'primitiveness' or 'sophistication' of the sign-system itself.

We have suggested that a consideration of the problem of the origins and evolution of the human architectonic system cannot be satisfactorily addressed without a consideration of communication and representation in general, as manifested in a wide variety of activities including gesture and spatiokinesis, speech, toolmaking, territoriality, and so forth. Each of these activities will necessarily supply important inputs to our understanding. Social communication comprises ensembles of mutually-reflective and transmuted sign-systems designed to function autonomously and in concert.

What we learn within one system will affect our understanding of all others. Conversely, our understanding of one is a function of our picture of the totality, including their cognitive contexts.

It appears to be the case, for example, as von Glasersfeld suggests, that the acquisition of communicating signs requires much the *same stage* of operational evolution as does toolmaking:

An analysis of tool making shows that it requires the operational capability, in the active organism, to isolate recorded clusters of sensory signals and to *detach them from the original cluster in order to set them up as reference values of a new feedback loop that becomes embedded in an existing one.* This detaching of recorded sensory coordinates constitutes the formation of a *representation*, and is the cybernetic equivalent of Piaget's analysis of the ontogeny of the 'permanent object' concept (italics D.P.) (von Glasersfeld 1976:223).

Human semiosis may very well distinguish itself from other zoo-semiotic behavior in the *complexity of its cross-modal systematicity*, and the multiply-recursive embeddedness of its representations. This transmutability, however, carries with it a concomitant referential consciousness of *particular* sensory modalities.

In other words, not only is human semiosis highly multimodal, it is also intensely inframodal. Semiotic systems behave in a semidetachable or semiautonomous fashion with respect to each other under conditions which may dampen or make inappropriate the use of one or more of the other available modalities. While it is present, the awareness of individual sensory modes is evidently considerably weaker among nonhumans, as von Glasersfeld suggests (von Glasersfeld 1976:216-217).

The picture of architectonic development painted above in Chapters II, III and IV suggests an equivalent perspective, involving analyses, syntheses, and reanalyses of percepts—a process of continual and cumulative separation and reembedding of percepts. An object, or cluster of sensory signals, will have become a reference item in its own right. In order to become a reference item, an object has to be cut loose from its original context, 'where it was a more or less relevant sensory adjunct to an activity cluster' (von Glasersfeld 1976:216), and it must have become something very like a *representation*—i.e. a cluster of recorded signals which, though originally composed of perceptual material, is no longer dependent on signals in the channels of sensory perception.

Such representations would have been cross-classified and made into components of hierarchically ordered systems serving in various ways (metaphorically, metonymically, synechdochally) as referential formations or *signantia*, in association with given *signata*.

TOWARDS A HOLISTIC MODEL OF CULTURE

The human grade of intelligence is such that when presented with a choice between two alternatives, we invent a third, or we answer a question with a question. The !Kung bushmen have a term for those who excel at this: they are called *t'xudi kaus*, 'masters of cleverness' (Yellen 1977:47). Over the course of hominid evolution, it has been the *t'xudi kaus* who have seen a larger proportion of their offspring reach reproductive age.

We are the result of this long process. Even by comparison with other advanced primates such as the chimpanzees, the modalities of human culture, while drawing on characteristic features manifest in the behaviors of other primates, have so transcended them, at some point in the very distant past, as to make the human cultural mode appear like a quantum jump.

By comparison, of course, it is, if we compare opposite ends of a spectrum directly to each other.

One of the primary aims of the foregoing has been to suggest a number of criteria and conditions for models of the emergence of the sociocultural way of life, from the perspective of one of its primary modalities, the system of the built environment. In terms of attempting to construct a holistic view of culture, we have sought to elaborate this perspective with an eye towards its cultural complement, verbal language, itself seen through a framework highlighting *shared* features of design. It has not been our aim in the present study to explicitly examine equivalent properties, a subject taken up in some detail elsewhere.[8]

But in attempting to maintain a cross-modal sensitivity, we have sought to highlight the fact that an understanding of culture itself must incorporate an integrated analysis of verbal and visual communication, representation and expression. In this we would concur with the view of G. Witherspoon, who notes that each culture

. . . has two principal symbolic systems: linguistic and nonlinguistic. The ideas and views of a people are embedded in and communicated by both symbol-systems, and it seems unfortunate that anthropologists interested in world view have seldom made a coordinated analysis of both systems. The native of a particular culture does not live, think and communicate in two different worlds. Linguistic and nonlinguistic symbols for a people who speak and use them form a single meaningful system, although each has its own particular emphases and uses. An analysis of a people's world view as seen through linguistic symbols and as seen through nonlinguistic symbols will not produce a single view of the same world. Each symbolic system provides a different device, a different angle, a different point of view. This difference, however, is not so much contradictory as it is complementary. Linguistic and nonlinguistic symbolic systems, for the most part, enhance and supplement each other (Witherspoon 1975:7).

This study has emphasized the view that the question of the origins and evolution of the one are inseparably bound up with those of the other, and that this is required both on the basis of their peculiar design features and characteristically cross-modal operant behaviors, and on the basis of their particularly strong cognitive interlinkages. Not only does each system incorporate elements whose meaningfulness cannot be entirely disambiguated without cross-modal switching, but social communicative acts characteristically embed each in the other, in dynamic synchronization. A communicative event is typically a dynamic, multimodal orchestration of each copresent acts.[9]

We are far from being able to elaborate satisfying formal models which purport to describe the evolution not only of culture itself but of its component ensembles or modalities of communication and symbolization,—assuming this to be a reasonably worthy goal in the first place, and apart from the fact that whatever is elaborated will only be temporarily satisfying anyway. As creatures designed for open-ended adaptability, we can only, to our good fortune, make things that leak.

Our principal footprint in the sand, culture, is the primary example of this. A culture is designed to be an open system, balancing stability with obsolescence. Whatever the processes involved in the emergence of human systems of social communication—and there are a variety of reasonable scenarios—one type of human emerged triumphant, radiating to all corners of the terrestrial biosphere while retaining its general somatic and cognitive uniformity. 'Speciation' in effect has been shunted to cultural organization itself, with its transfinite formative realizations.

A culture comprises ensembles of communicational and representational systems, resources of information of any conceivable kind, stored and signaled in any conceivable medium, as well as patterns of rules for the integration and cross-referencing of modal ensembles.

It consists, in a broad sense, of a multidimensional and multi-modal spatiotemporal network of associations whose systemic patterns (and whose contents) vary from one society to another. It seems sensible that the overall design features of cultures should reflect, and be reflected in, the organization of what we as observers characteristically may distinguish as distinct systems, ensembles or modalities. But such a reflection cannot, it also seems, be directly translational.

A culture must be flexible, changeable, and adaptable to any possible set of circumstances which humans get themselves into. It must be *inexhaustible* in some sense, and it should purport to encode or usefully model the universe of individual and group experience, and it must 'know' everything, or at least provide the means for learning anything. It must not be transcendible.

It cannot be a 'well-formed' system any more than its component ensembles. It is not homogeneous, although it may be useful to propose a uniform 'style' for certain reasons, as in the case of reifying the component features of an ideology, to serve as an enhanced signal of implicitly-held common attitudes. Such a formation may function phatically, conatively, and aesthetically, such as a legal codex.

No one individual can 'master' once and for all the entire set of informational resources stored by a culture, since for one thing every culture purports to offer a central perspective on the entire universe of human experience. Information is stored differently across individuals with varying social roles and occupations. It is not necessary for every individual in a society to be a plumber for a city to function, any more than it is necessary for everyone to know how to parent in order for the society to survive.

The cultural resources of a society are learned by individuals over time (in a process which remains unfinished at death). As an ordered system of resources, a culture is complexly organized, and in the growth of an individual the system is reconstructively generated in partly normative and partly idiosyncratic ways. (The very power of Hellenic—or indeed any other—divinities derived from their *deviant* ability to give rise to things full-blown from their brains, a property in evident marked (and deliberate) contrast to patent features of human learning.) Moreover, each new construct potentially offers a reevaluation of the universe of knowledge of a society or some portion of it in microscopic or macrocosmic ways.

What is known about one's culture is a function of viewpoint, perspective, or orientation, as well as the purpose to which informational resources are to be put. This must be so if a cultural way of life is to be adaptively useful to a maximum number of individuals. In effect, each modality as defined by a given culture should be able to be employed as a key to an understanding of the whole or to provide some momentarily relevant pathway through the forest of symbols.

Any portion of the resources of a culture is potentially a 'metalanguage' with respect to all other perceived portions, including itself. Consequently, a culture will have to be designed or 'packaged' in a hierarchically-ordered fashion so that is perspectives or modalities are temporarily partly autonomous and semi-detachable, and capable of illuminating or reading out an addressed context. Moreover, modalities should be designed so as to temporarily align with other modalities in extracting information.

A culture is not a machine, an organism, a semi-lattice, or a macromolecule. Its flexibility and potency are bought at the expense of rigid internal uniformity or homogeneity. Its component parts overlap in terms of their possibilities for usage, and they will offer partly redundant and alternative means for accomplishing ends which for the moment or over the long haul may be seen as isofunctional.

It would be wise to put to bed the question of the existence of value-neutral metalanguages which serve to unlock the geometry of the organization of cultural totalities. Neither ground nor figure are neutral, blank or unstructured.

To be sure, the position one takes with regard to an observed object, ensemble or network of relationships is not a matter of indifference normally. If one is interested in landing an instrument package on Mars or in understanding how it might be that the geological structure of the moon could illuminate the evolutionary history of the Earth, then a perspective on the situation which sees the planets as component parts of a stellar *system* with certain properties, then a model of the heavens with the Earth at the center rather than the sun will be less useful. That there are privileged perspectives or analytic stances is not at issue. But privilege is a function of the *purpose* to which evidence is to be put.

There are no absolute metalanguages to be discovered (verbal language, mathematics or vision need not apply), but rather—and much more interestingly—only *infralanguages* which are part and topologically-extended parcel of the operant behavior and organization of whatever set of percepts we have provisionally brought into our ken.

Having come into existence by whatever means and for whatever purpose, any piece of analysis is in some way metaphorically, metonymically, synechdochally, or ironically related to what is being focussed upon at a given time. Such a perspective forms both a model (representation) *of* and extension *to* the resources of a given ensemble, an addition to its body. An analysis or perspective, say, on verbal language (such as a formalized 'linguistics') is a 'singularity' of the conceptual space of language structure itself, like a wave on an ocean whose existence is in part a function of corresponding deformations and depressions in the surrounding topography of that conceptual space. As Jakobson notes,[10] the picture of language incorporates the sum and more of all language-like systems which have been evolved, including those which have evolved to examine language itself. The latter is altered by the addition to itself of even those analytic languages which have come about to talk about language itself.

The same will be true for all ensembles which a given culture will distinguish in the ordering of its resources. If this were *not* the case, we may surmise that a cultural way of life would have long ago ceased to be adaptively advantageous.

Here there is an apparent paradox, one which is in a sense built into the design of culture itself. For cultures to operate in flexible, economical, and efficient ways, then each of its ensembles should behave *as if* its perspective on the totality of experience was autonomous, primary or privileged, even if neither verbal language nor visual thinking[11] can be considered in fact the 'mathematics' of culture—any more than mathematics itself is value-neutral.

If we look at the ordering of the built environment from the perspective of verbal language, then it may very well be that the built environment can be decoded and read out *as if it were* a 'text'—since for whatever purpose such a stance is momentarily useful. Hence in specifying the organization of any one ensemble, it is necessary to be aware that the resultant view is such principally from a given perspective. If we exchange our rose-colored spectacles for polarized lenses, it's a different world. In culture X, built environments may be *verbally* classified in the same lexico-semantic domain as baskets and envelopes, whereas in culture Y, architectonic formations may be lexically classified along with sheep, goats, and other smelly things.

But recall the words of Witherspoon above: linguistic and non-linguistic (e.g. visual) symbol systems offer *complementary* perspectives on a world. A world view of a people comprises sets of interactively related ensembles, no one of which paints a complete picture. Moreover, each is unthinkable without the other.

Each semiotic system in a culture offers a conventional matrix or armature around which the remaining totality of a culture may be modeled. The verbal and visual codes provide a stereoscopic armature for communication, brought into focus by the extraordinary cross-modal orchestrational abilities of the human brain.

A culture is not packaged or designed as a text, or as a building or as a logical network, or as a kinship system. It is designed according to organizational features common to all of these, and more. Perhaps the most appropriate *metaphor* at the moment would be the assertion that a culture is designed as a model of the brain. But even such a metaphor is metonymically embedded in its object.

The sociocultural revolution (or synthesis, or coalescence) which evolved complex semiotic systems such as the built environment consisted of the cumulative elaboration of a singular kind of *logic* which represented the results of increasingly successful experiences in environmental adaptation and collaborative living. This logic is most lucidly manifested, in all human semiotic activity, in the dynamic complementarity of sense-discrimination vs. sense-determination, paradigmatic vs. syntagmatic structure, metonymy vs. metaphor, indexicality vs. iconism, all of which represent transformative realizations of the same conceptual oppositions.

NOTES

1. Discussed by E. Menzel and M. Johnson (1976:131-142).
2. In addition to Menzel and Johnson, see S. Chevalier-Skolnikoff (1976:173-211); E. von Glasersfeld (1976:212-226); R. K. Davenport (1976:143-149); J. Lancaster (1968:439-457); N. Geschwind (1964:155-169).
3. See J. Lancaster (1968); N. Geschwind (1965:237-294, 585-644).
4. See R. K. Davenport (1976:148).
5. See Menzel and Johnson (1976:131).
6. Discussed in detail above, Chapter III.
7. See E. Menzel and M. Johnson (1976:140).
8. See above, Chapters III and IV, and D. Preziosi (1979a, Appendix B).
9. See D. Preziosi (1979a, Appendix A); also the work of A. Kendon (1974:181-184, 1972).
10. As discussed in a public address at MIT, Cambridge, Mass., April 1977; see Jakobson and Waugh (i.p.).
11. See R. Arnheim (1971); on C. Levi-Strauss, see D. Sperber (1975).

7

Discussion

It may be that any search for 'origins' ultimately leads to enigma and to further and more pressing questions. And in the present study we may have arrived back where we started. But perhaps we may have begun to know the place where we started in a different way. Which, after all, may be the point.

If we press the question of the origins and evolution of the system of the built environment, we find apparent evidence for a system which looks indistinguishable from our own a third of a million years ago. Perhaps the real question here is whether or not this is surprising. Metonymically and metaphorically, moreover, the apparent organization of the Terra Amata environment might suggest the copresence of verbal language of the type with which we are familiar.

Let us attempt to be clear about our inferential pathways through these problems, and our reasons for focussing upon the site of Terra Amata as an exemplary formation.

With regard to the architectonic code, the evidence for the nature of the semiotic system at Terra Amata is partly internal and partly comparative. On the one hand, since it is the case that a 'technological' or material model of simplicity vs. complexity is not directly or necessarily iconic with respect to architectonic organizational sophistication (or lack thereof), then our proper evidential focus must be on organizational or systemic complexity. Seen from this perspective, the Terra Amata formation is evidently isomorphic in organization—it bears a conceptual 'family resemblance'—to our own contemporary formations. Furthermore, the constructional organization of the hut is such as to require a familiar degree of planning and conceptualization. This is a different matter from whether or not the material composition should survive more than a season (recall our discussions about 'permanence'), or whether other materials might be more 'suitable' to their purposes. The latter reflects our own cultural biasses, and in the face of any indication to the contrary, we shall have to assume that the Terra Amatans chose to do what they did as they did it.

There are two factors which might mitigate our picture of architectonic 'sophistication'. First, our analytic corpus is restricted to *one* (albeit recurrent) *formation*. It seems likely that the actual Terra Amata corpus would include other formations, including other kinds of formations, elsewhere and at other seasons.

On the other hand this need not be an important theoretical problem, since an architectonic code is not inherently tied to a fixed number of formations. A 'settlement' may consist of a single formation or millions. What is more to the point is the nature of the systemic organization of formations.

A second factor which might affect our picture is the fact that apparently we have only the *formal* component of an architectonic sign—i.e. its *signantia*. Many of its references will always elude us.

On the other hand, the *signata* may be reasonably reconstructed on the basis of archaeological and ethnographic comparison and contrast. In this respect, the distinctive component traces of the Terra Amata construct are apparently compatible with familiar contemporary component features which can, with greater or lesser assurance, be linked to known behavioral associations.

The latter, however, may itself be mitigated on theoretical and pragmatic grounds. With regard to these considerations, it will be clear that they are mutually implicative and supportive. On archaeological and ethnographic grounds, a given trace of a certain type has culture-specific associations, which are defined in relation to a network of culture-specific associations. Form X in culture Y differs from X' in culture Z (or in culture Y at time T^2). We cannot discern the *precise* referential associations of given traces at Terra Amata. Is the row of stones to the north of the hearth a windbreak, a skewer rank or an idol stand, or all three, or none?

On the other hand, given the system of formations, which we assume to be meaningful in some way(s), we can begin to specify some things regarding what a given form of the hut cannot have been.

Hence it is possible to suggest generic parameters on meaning and functional orientation of a given foundation which will exist in equilibration with other parameters addressed to other data. Thus if we cannot say for certain what a particular form had as its referential context—its usage(s)—we might be able (a) to suggest parameters on usage which may have been generically isofunctional with respect to parameters drawn from known contexts, and (b) to supply reasonable and context-sensitive hypotheses with respect to a form's functional 'orientation' (in the sense of Chapter III above) upon other-than-referential components of transmission. The latter considerations are often absent from, or confused in, much archaeological analysis.

The theoretical mitigating factors referred to above reflect an input from the study of architectonic semiosis *per se*, and, more broadly, from communicational behavior among humans in general. Because of the conventional and code-specific association between a formation and its referent(s), a given formation does not necessarily suggest the same referent(s) in a different context or code. What may look like a barber pole in code Q (because in code R it was) may in fact be a phallic fetish.

Theoretical and pragmatic considerations are mutually supportive, and it will be clear that even on theoretical grounds, in a system of communication and representation it would be maladaptive for anything to signify everything. Furthermore, as we have seen, a formation may be associated or linked to its referent(s) in a variety of ways—metaphorically, metonymically, synechdochally, ironically, either singly or (more characteristically) in combination.

It would appear, then, that we are left with the *evident fact* that the emergence of a system of social communication such as the architectonic code, as a system of visual communication and representation, is at least as early as a late *homo erectus* who had not yet fully evolved toward being *sapiens*.

Such a picture clearly raises a number of issues, not least of which being the question of what exactly the *sapiens* emergence comprised socioculturally.

We have taken as one of our working assumptions in this study that the emergence of the architectonic code necessarily occurred hand-in-hand with the emergence of verbal language as we now know it. This view is consonant with that of an increasing number of researchers, as we have noted. Such a position is required both on systemic and cognitive grounds. There patently exist, as we have noted in this study, common *features of design* in both systems, correlative processes of significative formation which transcend the enormous differences in medium, permanence, and geometries of address. These correlativities reflect a semiisofunctionality, partial redundancy, and mutuality of address in the two codes as systems of human social communication.

From such a standpoint, verbal language as we currently have it *ought* to have existed concurrently with the remains of the architectonic system of 300,000 B.P. But it is in fact the case that we need to know a great deal more about the *interactive behavior* of visual and vocal communication: as we have noted above, we need to study in much greater detail the ways in which each system supports the other in daily life, and particularly in constructional activity. When and how is verbal language needed to build a hut of the Terra Amata type, and what kind of language will suffice? It is perfectly possible that there will be a variety of alternative ways of exhorting one's fellows to go and collect sticks of a certain quantity and size.

On systemic grounds, it would appear at least plausible, and possibly necessary, that a vocal code built upon double articulation would be metonymically implicated by the existence of an architectonic code wherein component parts are, similarly, 'tools to make tools'.

Such a hypothesis might make hay of current glottochronological models which project the 'origins' of verbal language of the modern type much closer to us in time.[1] We again are directed to the problem of the *sapiens* emergence and the question of the *Neanderthalensis* relationship to the latter and to *homo erectus:* were the Terra Amatans Neanderthal?[2]

This problem is part of the broader issue of the relationship of brain-mass and 'cultural level'. There would undoubtedly have been a feedback effect of artifactual behavior upon somatic and cognitive evolution.[3]

The built environment of Terra Amata need not be an enigmatic isolate; there may be hundreds more to be uncovered. It need not have been a successful experiment. The system of the built environment may have emerged more than once, in many places. There may not be a direct geneology connecting Terra Amata and Dolni Vestonice. The builders and inhabitants of Terra Amata may have been *homo sapiens* whose progeny are invisible to us between then and the later Paleolithic. The *sapiens* grade of development may have been the result of conditions other than those which gave rise to architectonic (and, inferentially, linguistic?) systems. The built world of the Terra Amatans may have been fragile, unable to accommodate more complex social organizations, stratifications, and exogamous assimilations.

In short, we are faced with an enormous number of issues and possible scenarios. Our picture of the built world of the Terra Amatans is what we have taken to be an inference of the remains in the context of what we are able to infer from artifactual evidence of any kind. Our suggestion here is that on the basis of what we are presently able to understand about architectonic systems, and about social communication in general, there is nothing to completely dampen our pictures of the emergence of the built environment into its 'modern' human state in a very distant horizon, of which Terra Amata may then be at least a *terminus ante quem*.

This is by no means to imply that our understanding of visual semiosis is adequate or satisfactory. It is clear, however, that we are at the beginning of a journey, or at the beginning of a new and important phase of inquiry into the problem. The revelation of fundamental equivalencies in the *ways* in which architectonic and linguistic formations signify will have important ramifications in our understanding of social communication, and of culture itself. In the previous chapter, we sought to suggest that a culture is designed in ways which are homologous to the design of its component semiotic ensembles. Just as the units in a given code achieve their identity and definition through the interaction of an ordered network of relationships—i.e. through their systemic relationships —so also do whole codes or ensembles achieve definition through their intersystemic interaction. What constitutes a culturally meaningful code or ensemble is a function of how a particular culture orchestrates all of its semiotic resources relative to each other. The notion or *place* of 'language' or 'architecture' will be culture-specific in functionality, above and beyond whatever formal or structural isomorphisms exist among languages and built environments cross-culturally.

The study of the built environment is still partly embedded in the culture-specific and class-bound semantic maneuvering of prescriptive ideology. Even many contemporary 'semiotic' studies of architecture remain so entrapped.[4]

But the last thing which the development of an adequate architectonics needs is a clarion call for the rejection and dismantling of its ancestral art or architectural history. (Nor is the study of the conative or prescriptive aspect of the built environment to be completely sidestepped.) Some of the most powerful, lucid, and subtle analytic work in any field of endeavor has been carried out in an art historical framework by many generations of scholars of diverse backgrounds and interests.

We do not need to reinvent the wheel; we need to redesign a chassis to accommodate a functional engine.

In this endeavor, we need to understand many things. We need to understand more fully the nature of the various fundamental operant units in an architectonic code. We need to understand the nature of the 'boundaries' of each system, as well as the ability of individuals to code-switch or effectively use a new environment. We need to understand *in fine detail* the interactive dynamic synchronies of built environments with gestural signing, spatiokinetic display, and vocal language; that is to say we must seriously study *total* communicative events and the manifold ways in which individuals orchestrate signification in daily life. We need to understand *bricolage* in all modalities.

We need to know how built environments create and resolve visual illusion and ambiguity, and the precise nature of the perceptual-cognitive address to made objects. Our brains have been evolved (designed) in part to communicate linguistically; how have they been designed to also communicate visually and architectonically? Is there an innate 'grammar' of vision with a universal type of object-vocabulary?[5] We need to correlate the learning of visual or architectonic and linguistic distinctive features in childhood.[6]

How does a child in fact reconstruct the built environment of his elders? How is an architectonic code acquired?

We need to examine in greater detail the nature of architectonic signing *vis-à-vis* the roles of addresser and addressee, as well as the complexities of interrelationship between traditional sign-types such as icons, indexes, and symbols. We need to be clear about the relationship between architectonic systems and figurative and non-figurative 'art'.

In short, we need to know a great deal about things which are increasingly coalescent in terms of possible relevance. In a broad sense, we need to understand the relationship between built environment and cognitive organization.

The built environment uses as its signing medium anything and everything visually palpable. The apparent contrast with the singular vocal medium of verbal language is an artifact of a skewed focus. In both cases, the signing medium is a subset of the possible formations available in each channel, as realizable through the instrumentalities of that channel—the voice and ear, on the one hand, and the hand and eye, on the other.

A room, a sewing machine in the corner of the room, and the mountain on the horizon may become (however else the latter two may function) signs in a relational network of architectonic signs, according to the particular conventions of a given code.

The study of the built environment has more often than not focussed upon only two of its functions, the referential and the aesthetic, and this state of affairs, this way of dividing up the pie, has been confounded with time-and-culture-specific notions of what buildings ought to do and how they ought to do it (misconstruing conation, expression, phatic-territoriality, and allusory reference). The received confusion as to whether 'architecture' was 'art', craft, engineering, theater, or housing (or all, none, or some) is the result of folk-classification and bricolage having its origins in social and class perceptions of distinctions among referential object types.

Much of our received confusion has also stemmed from the very complexity and variety of the architectonic medium—which purely and simply is potentially coterminous materially with the entire set of resources offered by the surfaces of the planet. But the architectonic system is a system of relationships, not of forms or materials.

The architectonic and linguistic codes conceptually appropriate the world in its totality. And, in a mutually implicative fashion, they topologically incorporate each other. In their origins, functional structure, and operant behaviors they are stereoscopically inseparable. Any picture of human cognitive and symbolic origins which excludes one or the other, and which divorces both from the complex systems of sociocultural behavior in which they are necessarily embedded, is an academic fiction.

NOTES

1. On the subject in general, see R. L. Holloway (1976:330 ff.); H. J. Jerison (1976:370 ff.); and see especially J. T. Lamendella (1976:396 ff.).
2. See E. Lenneberg (1966) and E. H. Hess (1978:23 f., 43 f.).
3. See J. Bruner.
4. But see D. Agrest and M. Gandelsonas (1977:90-120).
5. If in fact there is, on internal and comparative grounds it can only be understood within the context of particular achitectonic codes; see D. Preziosi (1979a, Chapter I).
6. Perhaps the most urgent task awaiting visual semiotics. For a view of perception with important implications for semiotics, see J. Hochberg (1978); Neisser (1976). A discussion of the semiotic nature of visual perception will be found in the present writer's monograph 'Art, Semiosis and Perception', to appear. On the subject of child language acquisition, the most comprehensive and recent synthesis appears in R. Jakobson and L. R. Waugh (i.p.).

Bibliography

Agrest, D. and Gandelsonas, M. (1979), 'Semiotics and the limits of architecture', in *A Perfusion of Signs,* ed. by T. A. Sebeok, 90-120.

Alcock, J. (1972), 'The evolution of the use of tools by feeding animals', *Evolution* 26:464-473.

Altman, S. A., editor (1967), *Social Communication Among Primates.*

Arnheim, R. (1971), *Visual Thinking.*

_____ 1977), *The Dynamics of Architectural Form.*

Baran, H., editor (1976), *Semiotics and Structuralism: Readings from the Soviet Union.*

Basso, K. H. and H. A. Selby, editors (1976), *Meaning in Anthropology.*

Bower, T. G. R. (1977), *A Primer of Infant Development.*

Bruner, J. (1966), *Studies in Cognitive Growth.*

Chance, M. R. A. (1967), 'Attention structure as the basis of primate rank orders', *Man* 2:503-518.

Chance, M. R. A. and C. J. Jolly (1970), *Social Groups of Monkeys, Apes and Men.*

Chang, K.-C. (1970), *Settlement Archaeology.*

*The number of studies potentially relevant to the variety of issues raised in this book is enormous. The following list is restricted to all citations in the text, plus a number of additional items which may be useful not only for their content, but also for their often extensive bibliographies. Additional material of relevance to architectonic semiotics is listed in Preziosi 1979a. The abbreviation OELAS below refers to the volume under Harnad et al.

Chevalier-Skolnikoff, S. (1976), 'The ontogeny of primate intelligence and its implications for communicative potential', *OELAS*: 172-211.

Cohen, Y. A., editor (1968), *Man in Adaptation: the Biosocial Background.*

Collins, P. (1965), *Changing Ideals in Modern Architecture.*

Crick, M. (1976), *Explorations in Language and Meaning.*

Cunningham, C. (1964), 'Order in the Atoni house', *Bijdragen tot de Taal-, Land- en Volkenkunde* 120:34-68.

Davenport, R. K. (1976), 'Cross-modal perception in apes', *OELAS* 143 ff.

Douglas, M., editor (1973), *Rules and Meanings.*

de Lumley, H. (1966), 'Les fouilles de Terra Amata à Nice', *Bulletin du Musée d'Anthropologie prehistorique de Monaco* 13:29-51.

———— (1969), 'A Palaeolithic camp at Nice', *Scientific American* May:42 ff.

Eco, U. (1977), *A Theory of Semiotics.*

Fairservis, W. A. (1975), *The Threshold of Civilization.*

Foucault, M. (1972), *The Archaeology of Knowledge.*

Geshwind, N. (1964), 'Development of the brain and the evolution of language', *Monograph Series in Language and Linguistics* 17: 155-169.

———— (1965), 'Disconnection syndromes in animals and man', *Brain* 88:237-294, 585-644.

———— (1968), 'The development of the brain and the emergence of human language', in *Primates: Studies in Adaptation and Variability*, ed. by P. C. Jay, 439-457.

Giedion, S. (1971), *Architecture and the Phenomena of Transition.*

Goldin-Meadow, S., and H. Feldman (1977), 'The development of language-like communication without a language model', *Science* 197:401-402.

Gombrich, E. N., J. Hochberg, and M. Black (1972), *Art, Perception and Reality.*

Goodnow, J. (1977), *Children Drawing.*

Greenberg, J., editor (1966), *Universals of Language* second edition.

Harnard, S. R., H. D. Steklis, and J. B. Lancaster, editors (1976), 'Origins and evolution of language and speech', *Annals of the New York Academy of Sciences OELAS*: 280.

Hart, R. D. and G. T. Moore (1972), 'The development of spatial cognition', in *EDRA III: Proceedings of the IIIrd Environmental Design Research Conference, Los Angeles,* ed. by W. Mitchell.

Hawkes, T. (1977), *Structuralism and Semiotics.*

Haynes, R. (1970), 'Behavior space and perceptor space: a reconnaissance', in *Man-Environment Systems,* July.

Hill, J. (1974), 'Hominoid proto-linguistic capacities', in *Language Origins,* ed. by R. Wescott, 185 ff.

Holloway, R. L. (1976), 'Palaeoneurological evidence for language origins', *OELAS:* 330 ff.

Hochberg, J. (1972), 'The representation of things and people', in *Art, Perception and Reality,* 47-94.

_____ (1978), *Perception,* second edition.

Hockett, C. F. and R. Ascher (1964), 'The human revolution', *Current Anthropology* 5:135-147.

Honikian, B. (1972), 'An investigation of the relationship between construing the environment and its physical form', in *EDRA III: Proceedings of the IIIrd Environmental Design Research Conference, Los Angeles,* ed. by W. Mitchell.

Hymes, D. (1969), *Linguistic Models in Archaeology* (Mimeo).

_____ (1974a), *Reinventing Anthropology.*

_____ (1974b), *Foundations in Sociolinguistics.*

Jakobson, R. (1938), 'Observations sur le classement phonologique des consonnes', in *Proceedings of the IIIrd International Conference of Phonetic Sciences,* 39-41.

_____ (1956), 'Metalanguage as a linguistic problem', Presidential address to the Linguistic Society of America, December.

_____ (1960), 'Language and poetics', in *Style in Language,* ed. by T. A. Sebeok, 350-377.

_____ (1971a), 'Linguistic aspects of translation', *Selected Writings II,* 260 ff.

_____ (1971b), 'Shifters, verbal categories and the Russian verb', *Selected Writings II,* 130-147.

_____ (1975), *Coup d'Oeil sur le Developpement de la Semiotique.*

————— (1977), 'A few remarks on Peirce, pathfinder in the science of language'.

Jakobson, R. and M. Halle (1956), *Fundamentals of Language.*

Jakobson, R. and L. R. Waugh (i.p.), *The Sound Shape of Language.*

Jay, P. C. (1968), *Primates: Studies in Adaptation and Variability.*

Jencks, C., editor (1970), *Meaning in Architecture.*

Jerison, H. J. (1976), 'The palaeoneurology of language', *OELAS:* 370 ff.

Jespersen, O. (1922), *Language: Its Nature, Development and Origins.*

Jolly, C. J. (1972), *The Evolution of Primate Behavior.*

Kendon, A. (1972), 'Some relationships between body motion and speech: an analysis of an example', in *Studies in Dyadic Communication*, ed. by A. Siegman and B. Pope.

————— (1974), 'Kinesics, speech and language', in *Language Origins,* ed. by R. Wescott, 81-84.

Key, M. R. (1975), *Paralanguage and Kinesics (Nonverbal Communication) with a Bibliography.*

————— (1977), *Nonverbal Communication: A Research Guide and Bibliography.*

Key, M. R. and D. Preziosi, editors (i.p.), *Nonverbal Communication Today.*

Kohler, W. (1926), *The Mentality of Apes.*

Kubler, G. (1965), *The Shape of Time.*

Lamendella, J. T. (1976), 'Relations between the ontogeny and phylogeny of language: a neorecapitulationist View', *OELAS:* 396 ff.

Lancaster, J. B. (1968), 'Primate communicational systems and the emergence of human language', in *Primates: Studies in Adaptation and Variability*, ed. by P. C. Jay, 439-457.

————— (1975), *Primate Behavior and the Emergence of Human Culture.*

Leach, E. (1976), *Culture and Communication.*

Leakey, R. and R. Lewin (1977), *Origins.*

Leech, G. (1974), *Semantics.*

Lenneberg, E. (1966), *Biological Foundations of Language.*

Levi-Strauss, C. (1965), *Tristes Tropiques.*

———— (1966), *The Savage Mind.*

Lynch, K. (1960), *The Image of the City.*

———— (1975), *What Time is this Place?.*

Marcus, C. C. (1974), 'The house as symbol of self', in *Designing for Human Behavior*, 130-146.

Marshack, A. (1972), 'Cognitive aspects of Upper Palaeolithic engraving', *Current Anthropology* 13 (3-4):445-471.

———— (1972b), *The Roots of Civilization.*

———— (1976), 'Some implications of the Palaeolithic symbolic evidence for the origin of language', *OELAS:* 289-311.

Marshall, L. (1960), '!Kung bushman bands', *Africa* 30(4):342-343.

Mellaart, J. (1964), *Catal Huyuk.*

Menzel, E. and M. Johnson (1976), 'Communication and language organization in humans and other animals', *OELAS*: 131-142.

Merleau-Ponty, M. (1964), *Signs.*

Mitchell, W., editor (1972), *EDRA III: Proceedings of the IIIrd Environmental Design Research Conference, Los Angeles.*

Michotte, A. (1950), 'The emotions regarded as functional connections', in *Feelings and Emotions: the Moosehart Symposium.*

Mukařovský, J. (1936 [1970]), *Aesthetic Function, Norm and Value as Social Fact*, trans. by M. E. Suino. Michigan Slavic Contributions.

———— (1978), 'On the problem of functions in architecture', in *Structure, Sign and Function: Selected Writings of Jan Mukařovský*, ed. by J. Burbank and P. Steiner, 236 ff.

Neisser, U. (1976), *Cognition and Reality.*

Norberg-Schulz, C. (1965), *Intentions in Architecture.*

———— (1971), *Existence, Space and Architecture.*

———— (1977), *Meaning in Western Architecture.*

Panofsky, I. (1962), *Studies in Iconology.*

Peirce, C. S. (1921-1948), *Collected Writings I-IV.*

Petrovich, S. B. and E. H. Hess (1978), 'An introduction to animal communication', in *Nonverbal Behavior and Communication*, ed. by A. Siegman and S. Feldstein, 17-53.

Piaget, J. (1954), *Origins of Intelligence.*

———— (1955), *The Construction of Reality in the Child.*

———— (1963), *The Origins of Intelligence in Children.*

_____ (1970a), *Structuralism.*

_____ (1970b), *Genetic Epistemology.*

_____ (1973), *Main Trends in Interdisciplinary Research.*

_____ (1978), *Behavior and Evolution.*

Piaget, J. and B. Inhelder (1967), *The Child's Conception of Space.*

Preziosi, D. (1966), 'Cessavit deinde ars', *Athens Journal.*

_____ (1970), *LABRYS: Report on the Project on Architectural and Settlement Analysis at Yale University.* New Haven, Charlton Press.

_____ (1974), *Architecture and Cognition* (Mimeo).

_____ (1977), 'Toward a relational theory of culture', *Lacus III.*

_____ (1978a), 'Language and perception', *Lacus IV.*

_____ (1978b), 'The parameters of the architectonic code', *Ars Semeiotica* October.

_____ (1978c), 'Architectonic and linguistic signs', paper delivered to the *First International Conference on the Semiotics of Art,* Ann Arbor, Michigan, May 1978; to appear in Proceedings.

_____ (1978d), 'Multimodal communication'. Paper delivered to the *IIIrd Congress of the Semiotic Society of America,* Providence, October.

_____ (1979a), *The Semiotics of the Built Environment. Advances in Semiotics Series.* Indiana, Indiana University Press.

_____ (1979b), 'Hierarchies of signs in nonverbal semiosis', *Lacus V.*

Proshansky, H. M., W. H. Ittleson, and L. Rivlin, editors (1970), *Environmental Psychology.*

Rapoport, A. (1969), *House Form and Culture.*

_____ (1972), 'Australian aborigines and the definition of place', in *EDRA III: Proceedings of the IIIrd Environmental Design Research Conference, Los Angeles,* ed. by W. Mitchell.

Rykwert, J. (1976), *Adam's House in Paradise.*

Sauer, C. O. (1962), 'Seashore—primitive home of man?', *Proceedings of the American Philosophical Society* 106(1):41-47.

Savan, D. (1976), 'An introduction to C. S. Peirce's semiotics', *Toronto Semiotic Circle Working Papers* (1).

Schapiro, M. (1972), *Words and Pictures.*

Schmandt-Besserat, D. (1973), 'An archaic recording system and the origin of writing', *Syro-Mesopotamian Studies* 1(2) (July).
———— (1978), 'The earliest precursor of writing', *Scientific American* 238(6):50 ff.
Sebeok, T. A. (1960), *Style in Language*.
———— (1965), 'Animal communication', *Science* 147(3661): 1006 f.
———— (1967), 'Discussion of communicational processes', in *Social Communication among Primates*, ed. by S. A. Altman.
———— (1968), *Animal Communication: Techniques of Study and Results of Research*.
———— (1972), *Perspectives in Zoosemiotics*.
Sebeok, T. A., editor (1977), *A Perfusion of Signs*.
Siegman, A. and S. Feldstein, editors (1978), *Nonverbal Behavior and Communication*.
Siegman, A. and B. Pope, editors (1972), *Studies in Dyadic Communication*.
Silverstein, M. (1976), 'Shifters, linguistic categories, and cultural description', in *Meaning in Anthropology*, ed. by K. H. Basso and H. A. Selby, 11-56.
Simons, E. L. (1972), *Primate Evolution*.
Sperber, D. (1975), *Rethinking Symbolism*.
Tambiah, S. J. (1969), 'Animals are good to think and good to prohibit', *Ethnology* 8(4):424-459.
Toporov, V. N. (1976), 'Toward the origin of certain poetic symbols: the Palaeolithic period', in *Semiotics and Structuralism: Readings from the Soviet Union*, ed. by H. Baran, 184-225.
Tuan, I.-F. (1975), *Topophilia*.
van Lawick-Goodall, J. (1971), *In the Shadow of Man*.
von Frisch, K. (1974), *Animal Architecture*.
von Glasersfeld, E. (1976), 'The development of language as purposive behavior', *OELAS*: 212-226.
Wallis, M. (1975), 'Semantic and symbolic elements in architecture', in *Arts and Signs*, 39-58.
Washburn, S. L. and R. Moore (1974), *Ape into Man: A Study of Human Evolution*.
Waugh, L. R. (1977), *Roman Jakobson's Science of Language*.
———— (i.p.), 'Marked and unmarked: a choice between unequals in linguistic and semiotic structure', *Semiotica*.

Waugh, L. R. and R. Jakobson (1979), *The Sound Shape of Language.*

Weinreich, U. (1966), 'On the semantic structure of language', in *Universals of Language,* second volume, ed. by J. Greenberg.

Wescott, R., editor (1974), *Language Origins.*

Wilson, E. (1975), *Sociobiology.*

Witherspoon, G. (1975), *The Central Concepts of Navajo World View.* Peter de Ridder Press Publications in World View I.

Yellen, J. (1977), *Archaeological Approaches to the Present: Models for Reconstructing the Past.*